WHO IS THE CHURCH?

WHO IS THE CHURCH?

AN ECCLESIOLOGY FOR THE TWENTY-FIRST CENTURY

CHERYL M. PETERSON

Fortress Press
Minneapolis

WHO IS THE CHURCH?

An Ecclesiology for the Twenty-First Century

Unless otherwise noted, scripture quotations are from the New Revised Standard Version Bible, copyright © 1989 by the Division of Christian Education of the National Council of Churches of Christ in the USA, and are used with permission.

Cover design: Laurie Ingram

Cover photo: Lazurite House. Copyright © 2012, Irina V. Brynza, Alpen Art Studio, www.etsy.com/shop/AlpenArtStudio

Library of Congress Cataloging-in-Publication Data

Print ISBN: 978-0-8006-9881-2

eBook ISBN: 978-1-4514-2638-0

The paper used in this publication meets the minimum requirements of American National Standard for Information Sciences—Permanence of Paper for Printed Library Materials, ANSI Z329.48-1984.

Manufactured in the U.S.A.

This book was produced using PressBooks.com, and PDF rendering was done by PrinceXML.

CONTENTS

Acknowledgments

One of the joys of writing this book is the opportunity to thank the many persons who helped bring it to publication. As with many first books, this one started out as a dissertation for the PhD degree at Marquette University, "The Question of the Church in North American Lutheranism: Toward a Theology of the Third Article" (2004). I want to thank the members of my dissertation committee (Patrick Carey, Michael Fahey, Bradford Hinze, and Markus Wriedt) for their encouragement and feedback. Special thanks to my dissertation director, D. Lyle Dabney, for his guidance and support throughout this project, and in particular for suggesting that I start my ecclesiology with the Holy Spirit and for proposing a narrative method for doing so. I also want to thank former Fortress Press editor-in-chief, Michael West, for his help in thinking through how my dissertation might be transformed into a publishable book.

I am deeply grateful to many other academic colleagues who read the proposal and/or individual chapters and offered critical feedback: Amy Carr, Brian Flanagan, Jason Fout, Bradford Hinze, Donald Huber, and Mark Allan Powell. Thanks also to Philip Butin for the helpful conversation about this theological project. I wish to offer special and heartfelt thanks to Lynn Kauppi and Matthew Kruse who read the whole manuscript and offered invaluable suggestions for improvement in the text itself and overall flow of the argument. I also want to thank my editor at Fortress Press, David Lott, for his helpful revisions and suggestions for reshaping the manuscript into its final form.

I appreciated the opportunity to present many of my ideas at both academic and ecclesial conferences during the writing of this book, including two seminars of the Lutheran World Federation, "The Church in the Midst of Empire" (St. Paul, Minnesota, 2007), and "The Marks of the Church" (Bossey, Switzerland, 2008); the Convocation of Evangelical Lutheran Church in America (ELCA)/Evangelical Lutheran Church in Canada Teaching Theologians (2010); the Northern Rockies Institute of Theology (2012); as well as a number of gatherings for rostered leaders in various ELCA Synods: Central States (2008), Northwestern Ohio (2011), Upper Susquehanna (2011), Southwestern Minnesota (2011), and South Central Synod of Wisconsin (2011). Participants' questions and comments helped me to sharpen my constructive proposal and to begin exploring the practical application of my ideas. I want especially to thank the pastors (and Trinity alumni) who shared stories and resources from their own ministry contexts, many of which were included in the epilogue: Rick Barger, Epiphany Lutheran Church in Suwanee, Georgia; Kate Davidson, Hope Lutheran Church in Clinton, Maryland; Matthew Kruse, Redeemer Lutheran Church, Rio, Wisconsin; and Kevan Penvose, Unity Lutheran Church, Milwaukee.

Finally, I wish to thank all who supported the writing of this book, especially the Wabash Center for Teaching Religion and Theology for their 2009 Summer Fellowship, my faculty colleagues at Trinity Lutheran Seminary, and other friends and colleagues too numerous to name.

This book came to fruition as my husband, Chuck, was finishing his dissertation for the PhD degree in philosophy from Marquette University. It was not always easy living in a "two-book household," but I could not have finished this book without his love and support. I dedicate this book to him.

Introduction: Asking the Right Question

On the thirty-fifth anniversary of the radio show *A Prairie Home Companion*, host Garrison Keillor interviewed a Lutheran pastor in the town of Avon, Minnesota, where the show was being broadcast that night. The pastor served a multipoint parish, three congregations (all with Norwegian roots) that were four to five miles apart from each other and where the median age of the members was sixty to seventy years old.[1] Keillor asked the obvious question, "Have you brought up the subject of consolidation?" The pastor sheepishly said, "Well, we have beautiful cemeteries around each church, and we . . ." Keillor interrupted him with the retort: "It says in Scripture, Pastor, that the dead shall bury the dead."

We are living in a time when survival is on the mind of most mainline congregations and denominations. The viability of the mainline churches is being questioned in nearly every corner of the church, with some prognosticators even predicting their demise. One analyst has forecast that, given certain trends and demographics, my denomination, the Evangelical Lutheran Church in America, will "turn out the lights" in 2046.[2] Others challenge this prediction, arguing for the ultimate resilience and viability of the mainline churches in these changing times.[3] Either way, it is an undeniable fact that the mainline churches in the United States are in a significant numerical decline.[4]

Since the 1960s, numerous articles and books addressing this phenomenon have appeared, trying to get a handle on why the mainline churches are declining in members and influence.[5] In 1972, Dean Kelley argued in his book *Why Conservative Churches Are Growing* that "mainline decline" could be attributed to its liberal (and therefore, in his view, accommodating) theology, because at the same time these churches were shrinking, conservative churches, which offered a much more rigid and strict set of beliefs and moral codes, were growing. Kelley's theory is still popular[6] but it has been challenged by sociologists and church leaders who point to changing fertility rates and other cultural factors as the primary culprits.[7]

Whatever the cause(s), this decline is causing great fear and anxiety in the mainline churches. This is due not only to the fact that these churches are growing numerically smaller, but also because they have lost a certain cultural and social position within American society and are becoming "sideline"[8] churches, a situation that evangelicals may be facing sooner rather than later as well.[9] The findings of a 2008 study by the American Religious Identification Survey (ARIS) confirm conclusions reached in earlier studies: "Americans are slowly becoming less Christian and . . . in recent decades the challenge to Christianity in American society does not come from other world religions or new religious movements (NRMs) but rather from a rejection of all organized religions."[10]

These statistics reflect a trajectory to which Douglas John Hall and others have been pointing for years. This is the shift from a *de facto* form of Christendom that has been operative in various guises in the United States since its founding, but which flourished in a new way in the American Enlightenment. The optimistic narrative of a Christian America gave the Protestant churches a clear role and purpose in society with no concerns about survival. Since the 1960s, mainline churches have found themselves being "disestablished" (Hall's term) and losing a clearly defined role and sense of identity in the larger social fabric.

RESPONSES TO MAINLINE DECLINE

The crisis of the mainline decline is on the minds of most congregation members, but not everyone is on the same page about what it means and what ought to be done about it. Pastors and other leaders are looking for resources to help them respond to this changing situation. Various books and programs continue to appear, promising to do just this. The underlying question of most of these strategies seems to be: "What shall we do to turn this situation around?" These strategies see the primary issue as one of membership decline and propose solutions to do something different so that congregations survive and perhaps even thrive in this changing context.

Some churches are simply trying to "market" themselves and their message in light of the changing realities. This seems to be the major strategy of Leonard Sweet and others in the church-growth movement. This strategy, which church consultant Reggie McNeal and others have dubbed "attractional evangelism," involves understanding the culture and its needs in order to be better able to address what churches have to offer the culture. The goal is to draw people back into churches by offering programs that serve people's needs (a strategy McNeal refers to—and criticizes—as "if you build it, they will come") and by letting people know how the gospel is relevant to their lives.[11]

Others charge that simply bringing more people in the doors is not the solution; we need to "do" church differently. The problem isn't just the message—it is the form in which the message comes. The so-called emerging-church movement grew out of a reaction to the church-growth movement as a way to explore new ways of being and doing church that are more authentic and relational. This strategy recognizes that many people see the church primarily as an organization or social club and, therefore, as increasingly irrelevant to their lives. Yet, emerging-church leaders interpret that people are not looking to "join" organizations; they are looking for authentic community and deep spiritual experiences. Others outside of the emerging-church movement have noted this trend as well. While interest in spirituality is on the rise, many of these spiritual seekers are looking elsewhere, because, as Diana Butler Bass argues in her book *Christianity after Religion*, they are not finding the authentic community they seek in traditional congregations.[12] McNeal proposes that is because most mainline churches are more secular than the culture that surrounds them. In fact, McNeal charges that most mainline church culture—with its emphasis on membership over discipleship—is not "spiritual enough" to help people with the questions they are asking about life and God: "The problem is that when people come to church, expecting to find God, they often encounter a religious club holding a meeting where God is conspicuously absent."[13] McNeal and others propose that an "incarnational" (as opposed to an "attractional") model of outreach offers the churches a way not only to share but also *to embody* the relevancy of the gospel to the questions of peoples' lives.

Finally, Christianity's increasingly negative image problem presents a difficulty that goes beyond simple irrelevancy. The evangelical authors of *unChristian: What a New Generation Thinks about Christianity and Why It Matters* offer a statistical analysis about what "outsiders" think of evangelical Christianity: they see Christians as hypocritical, antigay, sheltered and out of touch, too political, judgmental, and ultimately only worried about getting more converts in order to survive.[14] Many liberal mainline congregations are seeking to become places of "radical hospitality" in response to the negative images of Christianity and the postmodern concern for authentic community. Recent ad campaigns, such as the United Church of Christ's "God is Still Speaking,"[15] have aimed especially at people outside of the church who have a negative view of the church as, for instance, doctrinally and morally rigid.

A related solution to *doing something different* is for the church to *rediscover its purpose*. In this view, the problem underlying the current ecclesial crisis is simple: we do not know what the church is for. This solution, which Rick Warren has popularized in his best-selling books *The Purpose-Driven Church* and *The Purpose-Driven Life*,[16] involves discerning (or finding) a single purpose for one's ministry or life. As Jonathan Wilson notes, however, even though *The Purpose-Driven Church* begins by asserting "it's not about you," the clear thesis of the book "is that it is about you and your fulfillment."[17] The ecclesiology implied in *The Purpose-Driven Church* is made explicit in *The Purpose-Driven Life*: that the church is instrumental to the fulfillment of individuals, making Warren's proposal not that different from other church-growth strategies.

Who Is the Church?

Whether the assumption is that the churches have lost their marketability, relevance, credibility, authenticity, or purpose, these solutions take as a given that the problem is membership decline and the solution is to find the right strategies to address this. What can we do to turn this situation around? What can we do to bring people back into the churches again? What can we do to get the church to grow and thrive again in this changing context? *What shall the church do?*

I suggest that this question, "What shall we do?" and its correlates, "What is the church for?" and "Why the church?," while not irrelevant to the situation facing the churches, nonetheless should not be asked apart from a prior, more basic question. The mainline churches *are* facing an ecclesial crisis, but it is much more than a crisis of declining numbers and membership. There is a deeper and more basic issue that must be explored, one that has to do with the church's theological identity, that is, *what it means to be the church*. It is my thesis that the church today is facing *an identity crisis*. It is not simply that the church is culturally irrelevant or inauthentic; these are symptoms of the underlying issue, which is that *we don't know who we are as church*. Thus I propose that rather than searching for solutions and strategies, the churches need to wrestle vigorously with the question, *Who is the church?* This is a theological question that calls for a theological answer.[18]

At the same time, a theological investigation of the church's identity cannot be done in a historical and social vacuum. It is necessarily contextual. To answer the question "Who is the church?" requires attention to the context in which the church finds itself. According to Roman Catholic theologian Nicholas Healy, "Ecclesiology is not about the business of finding the right way to think about the church, of developing a blueprint suitable for all times and places . . . but to aid the concrete church in performing its task of witness and pastoral care within what I call its 'ecclesiological context.'"[19] This includes attention not only to the current context in which the church finds itself, but also the historical background of that context. Who we are as the church also requires that we ask, "How did we get here in terms of our thinking about the church?"

Thus the difficulty is not simply that the aforementioned strategies do not explicitly address the question of the church's identity. An investigation of the historical context will show the larger problem: these strategies *already presume* a concept of the church, one that can be characterized as a "voluntary association." Further, I will show that this concept is the *de facto* American ecclesiology and *itself part of the identity crisis*. Most mainline Protestants in this country—regardless of what their traditions theologically teach about the doctrine of the church—operate *in practice* with a view of the church as a voluntary association of self-selecting individuals. This concept is centered on the individual and his or her choice to affiliate (or not) with a particular congregation, denomination, or even a "nondenominational" entity, rather than on the Triune God who calls, gathers, enlightens, and sends the church. As we have seen, the majority of responses to the ecclesial crisis of the mainline churches are given with this paradigm in mind, focusing on what individuals want or need and how to attract individuals to the church. This is an anthropological, even sociological, rather than a theological concept of the church.

At the same time, I agree with those theologians who believe that methodologically, ecclesiology is a systematic task that begins "from below" in contrast to "from above." Whereas an ecclesiology from above attempts to give an account of the "essential nature and structure of the church that transcends any given context,"[20] an ecclesiology from below begins with the church's agency and its concrete ecclesial practices. Nicholas Healy posits that because "the church's life takes concrete form in the web of social practices accepted and promoted by the community as well in the activities of its individual members," it is therefore "not unreasonable to describe the concrete church, at least initially, in terms of agency rather than in terms of being."[21] For Healy, beginning with the church's agency is thoroughly theological because the church's activity is constituted by the activity of the Holy Spirit, which animates it. Healy proposes beginning with the apostolic task and the making of disciples.

Even if we begin with these basic tasks, I submit that the church needs to be a certain kind of community of people in order to accomplish these tasks faithfully. Again, the prior question remains one of identity. While I appreciate

Healy's focus on the Holy Spirit as the source of the church's *agency*—that is, what enables the church to act as God's people in the world—I propose we also consider the Spirit as the source of the church's *identity*. I therefore propose an "ecclesiology from below" that begins with the agency of the Holy Spirit *itself* in the movement of God's economy known as the *missio Dei*—the "mission of God"—which in turn gives the church its distinctive identity.

A central claim of this book is that the church finds its identity in the activity of the Holy Spirit. This makes the starting point for ecclesiology the Triune God and what God is doing, rather than the church and what its members do. Because of the peculiar history of American ecclesiology and the predominance of the voluntary association concept, it is especially important to begin with God and God's activity in addressing the doctrine of the church in this context.

It is also methodologically useful in that it allows a way around the "functional versus ontological" impasse that seems to plague much Protestant conversation about the doctrine of the church. Historically, Lutherans and many other Protestants have preferred to define the church by what "happens" in the assembly of those whom God gathers: the proclamation of the word and the administration of the sacraments. The church's "being" is rooted in what happens in the gathered assembly, that is, God speaks the word of promise. Later Lutheran theologians refer to this as a "word-event" concept of the church. The historic Protestant concern with ontology has to do with how the church's being is related to God's being, a concern that has traditionally played out in terms of monistic and hierarchal concepts (and structures) of the institutional church. In particular, these concerns have focused on Thomistic ideas of an analogy of being and not with the question of ontology itself, which simply means an accounting of something's nature or existence. Many ecumenically minded Protestants have begun to embrace a new ecclesiological paradigm that has emerged since the mid-twentieth century, one that interprets the being of the church in terms of God's trinitarian being as a communion of persons, understood in terms of a relational ontology. Ecclesial communion is modeled on the idea of the communion of persons within the Trinity and is experienced horizontally as well as vertically.

EXPLORING ECCLESIAL PARADIGMS

One goal of this volume is to place the integrally interrelated questions of the church's identity and purpose at the center of a systematic inquiry of the church's nature: by comparing and contrasting the emerging missional paradigm of the doctrine of the church with these two important ecclesial paradigms from the last century: the neo-Reformation concept of the church as a "word-event" (where the starting point is the proclamation of the word that justifies the sinner) and the ecumenical paradigm of the church as "communion" (where the starting point is the immanent Trinity as a communion of persons).

The missional paradigm proposes that the church find its identity *in* God's mission: the church's identity is rooted in its participation in the mission of God, defined in terms of God's own trinitarian being, that is, a sending God. Because God is a missional God, the church is by nature a missional community, sent out as well as gathered by God's activity. It has become commonplace to contrast a "missional" ecclesiology with the ecclesiological framework of the Reformers; however, the vast amount of literature on ecumenical ecclesiology and its central paradigm of communion (*koinonia*) has not been taken into serious consideration in the same way by most of these authors. This is in spite of the fact that ecumenical dialogues have been the arena in which theologians (Protestant as well as Catholic and Orthodox) have engaged most "ecclesiology proper" over the last several decades. The important contributions of this paradigm—not least of all its emphasis on relationship and reconciled diversity—as well as its limitations should be engaged in the search for a contextual ecclesiology.

Thus, while I will preference the *missio Dei* paradigm by using it as a starting point, I am not choosing it over and against the other two paradigms. The goal of this book is not to argue for a new "blueprint ecclesiology," but to offer an approach to the question of the church ("Who is the church?") that addresses the "ecclesiological context" in which churches find themselves today. Each of these paradigms has something to contribute to the task at hand. My proposal draws on the strengths of all three. My contribution, then, is not to argue for one paradigm, but to offer a new approach to the question of the church's identity that not only integrates the strengths of these three major paradigms but does so by specifically "starting with the Spirit" and using a narrative method to do so. The idea of "starting with the Spirit" is not original to me,[22] but a unique contribution I offer is to bring together a pneumatological focus with a narrative method. I have argued that the question "Who is the church?" must be answered first by examining who God is and what God is doing. Rather than beginning with the *immanent* Trinity, I suggest beginning with the actual historical community of the church as narrated in Scripture as it relates to the work of the Trinity in the economy of salvation, that is, the *economic* Trinity. Thus a *narrative method* is most proper to the exploration of the church's identity. I propose that the question of the church's identity and purpose can best be answered in today's context by returning to the "story of the church," which properly "starts with the Spirit." To discover "who" the church is, we must begin with the story of the church in the Scriptures. A narrative method allows in this task a rich engagement with the Scriptures and, as I will argue, by extension the ecumenical creeds of the church as narrative summaries of Scripture.

I refer to my constructive approach with the designation "Spirit-breathed church." The phrase "Spirit-breathed" heretofore has been used to describe a view of the Holy Scriptures (based on 2 Tim. 3:16), but a narrative reading of the Scriptures would suggest it more appropriate to use this descriptor for the church. The image comes from John 20, sometimes called the Johannine Pentecost, which specifically includes Jesus giving the disciples a missionary charge: "As the Father has sent me, so I send you." The Spirit that Jesus breathes onto his disciples is the same Spirit that raised him from the dead (Rom. 8:11), to give them an identity and purpose as a people whose primary calling is not to "bury the dead" but to walk in the new life of the resurrection and be sent out to bear witness to the life-giving power of the gospel of Jesus Christ.

OUTLINE OF THE BOOK

In this study I discuss (1) the history of American mainline Protestant ecclesiology; (2) two paradigms important to my analysis; (3) the emergence of and significance of the "missional ecclesiology"; (4) the use of narrative analysis in ecclesiology; and (5) conclude with my proposal based upon a missional, narrative analysis of the Third Article of the Apostles' and Niceo-Constantinopolitan (Nicene) creeds. Thus the outline of the book is as follows:

Chapter 1 reviews in broad brushstrokes the story of mainline Protestant ecclesiology in the colonies and in the United States, from the Puritans to the present day. To explore the development of ecclesiological paradigms in the United States, I use the heuristic device of "What question(s) shapes the church's self-understanding?" These questions will be discussed alongside the cultural establishment of Christianity and the narrative of a "Christian America" that increasingly became intertwined with an ideology of progress. I also discuss the development of the voluntary principle and the role it played in enabling the mainline churches to view their identity in this larger narrative. I also review how the process of the church's disestablishment in the twentieth century has challenged the church's identity in this narrative. In engagement with Douglas John Hall and others, I examine how our post-Christendom context and its questions offer the churches an opportunity to face the crisis in which they find themselves.

Chapters 2 and 3 examine two contemporary ecclesiological paradigms—"word-event" and "communion"—that offer theological starting points for the task at hand as well as both important contributions and some shortcomings. For the first paradigm, which chapter 2 explores in detail, the question of the church's being or nature can only be recognized by what happens in its midst, that is, the proclamation of the word and the administration of the sacraments. This paradigm understands the being of the church in terms of event. There is less interest in *what* the church is as much as *what it does* (or, more properly, what God does in it), which can reduce the church to functional terms. My examination of the word-event paradigm is typified by Karl Barth and the more recent voices of the late Lutheran theologian Gerhard Forde and Reformed theologian Michael Horton.

The second paradigm, the subject of chapter 3, locates the being of the church in the divine life of the Triune God: the church is the body of Christ, a mystical communion, an organism through which members participate in the divine life, most centrally in the celebration of the Eucharist. The nature of the church as a "communion" is related to the very being of God—the "what" question is more central here. Ecclesial communion is modeled on the communion of the three persons within the Trinity and has vertical and horizontal dimensions. It is interpreted in terms of participation in the Triune God, whereby believers are brought into communion with the Triune God (and with one another) through their incorporation into the body of Christ through the sharing of the Lord's Supper. This chapter will discuss and critically evaluate this paradigm by examining the ecclesiologies of Lutheran theologian Robert W. Jenson and Reformed theologian Philip W. Butin.

While each paradigm has much to commend it, the chief difficulty with each is the presumption of a *de facto* Christendom context that has shaped both the "questions" being asked the church and the way those are answered. And so, with the change in the context and culture, we must critically engage the questions from this new sociological and theological location. A second, related concern is that while each paradigm has as its starting point God's agency, each tends to focus on the action of God to *gather* the church—so that its members can hear the promise and be united with God in Christ through the sacrament—but not also the action of God to *send* the church. Because these paradigms developed under Christendom, there is a danger of focusing on the first movement, the Spirit's gathering of the church, to the neglect of the second and consequently losing the missional aspect of the church's identity.

Chapter 4 will discuss the historical emergence of the missional paradigm, especially as it has developed in the work of the Gospel and our Culture Network and specifically in the work of two of its leading theologians, Darrell Guder and Craig Van Gelder. The *missio Dei* paradigm takes the post-Christendom context clearly into account in a way that the other two paradigms generally do not. Understood correctly, it also offers a helpful theological starting point from which to address the church's identity in our current context.

In taking up the *missio Dei* as the theological starting point for an "ecclesiology from below" (but one that also draws aspects from the previous two paradigms), I do so with two additional methodological moves that form the crux of my constructive proposal: the use of a narrative method and a pneumatologically focused reading of that narrative. The prior question being asked of the church in the post-Christendom context is not "What does the church do?" (a question about the church's function or purpose) or even "What is the church?" (a question about the church's nature or being), but "*Who* is the church?" To my knowledge, however, no one has yet attempted a narrative missional ecclesiology that "starts with the Spirit." This is especially surprising, considering not only the contemporary context but also the natural connection between the Spirit with the church in the New Testament narrative, especially the Acts of the Apostles, and in the ecumenical creeds.

The first part of chapter 5 will address the use of narrative as a method for ecclesiology. I will consider George Lindbeck's proposal for ecclesiology as a starting point for proposing my own: an exploration of the church's story arc in the Scriptures that "starts with the Spirit," specifically focusing on the church's identity and mission as narrated in the Acts of the Apostles. While this biblical book has begun to appear in resources for the "missional church," many mainline Christians have long been suspicious of Acts because of its association with church-growth movements and Pentecostalism, fearing it will lead to a theology of glory. This need not be the case if one understands the work of the Holy Spirit in a trinitarian framework. One way to do this is to show that my constructive proposal for a narrative, pneumatological, and missional ecclesiology is grounded not only in a fresh reading of Scripture, but also in the tradition of the church. This continuity with the historic church and its ecumenical creeds explicitly distinguishes my proposal from a more traditional Pentecostal approach.

In chapter 6, I consider the narrative of the church as it appears in the Apostles' Creed. Following the trinitarian framework of Martin Luther's treatment of the Apostles' Creed (in his Small and Large Catechisms), one can posit a "narrative" that runs through the creed and the Third Article in particular which shows these linkages and at the same time can serve as a framework for understanding the *church's Spirit-breathed identity and purpose*. Finally, I examine the classic "marks of the church" (one, holy, catholic, and apostolic) in the other historic catholic creed (the Niceo-Constantinopolitan) as further identifiers of the church's character. These marks, which have long been used to define the nature of the church, will be explored here as Spirit-breathed attributes of the church's narrative identity in a post-Christendom context.

I conclude with an epilogue that offers a snapshot of what a "Spirit-breathed church" might look like today and briefly explores how church leaders might apply these ideas in their own congregational settings.

For Reflection and Discussion

1. What responses to "mainline decline" have you seen tried in your congregation? Your denomination?
2. Do you agree that the church is facing an identity crisis, and not just a "numbers" crisis? How does asking the question, "Who is the church?" instead of "What shall we do?" change how you think about the situation facing the mainline churches?
3. The author considers three ecclesial paradigms in this book (word-event, communion, *missio Dei*). What are some other ecclesial paradigms or theological starting points for a doctrine of the church? Which ones have shaped your theological understanding of the church?
4. What is your first reaction to the idea of a "Spirit-breathed church?"

Notes

1. The interview can be heard online at http://prairiehome.publicradio.org/www_publicradio/tools/media_player/popup.php?name=phc/2009/07/04/phc_20090704_64&starttime=01:08:05&endtime=01:43:57.

2. Cited in Mark Hanson, "The Future of Lutheran Institutions," address given in January, 2005, https://archive.elca.org/bishop/messages/m_ELCAInstitutionsJan2005.pdf.

3. For example, Robert Bacher and Kenneth Inskeep, *Chasing Down a Rumor: The Death of Mainline Denominations* (Minneapolis: Augsburg, 2005).

4. Barry A. Kosmin and Ariela Keysar, "American Religious Identification Survey (ARIS 2008) Summary Report," March, 2009, 6, http://commons.trincoll.edu/aris/files/2011/08/ARIS_Report_2008.pdf.

5. Benton Johnson, Dean R. Hoge, and Donald A. Luidens discuss several theories in "The Mainline Church: The Real Reason for Decline," *First Things* 31 (March 1993): 13–18, http://www.leaderu.com/ftissues/ft9303/articles/johnson.html.

6. Joseph Bottum, "The Death of Protestant America: A Political Theory of the Protestant Mainline," *First Things* 185 (August/September 2008): 23–33, http://www.firstthings.com/article/2008/08/001-the-death-of-protestant-america-a-political-theory-of-the-protestant-mainline-19.

7. Michael Hout, Andrew Greeley, and Melissa Wilde, "Demographics of Mainline Decline: Birth Dearth," *The Christian Century* (October 4, 2005), 24–27.

8. Douglas John Hall, *Professing the Faith: Christian Theology in a North American Context* (Minneapolis: Fortress Press, 1993), ix.

9. This is noted with some irony in an editorial in *Christianity Today*: "The New (Evangelical) Mainline," *Christianity Today* (May 12, 2009), http://www.christianitytoday.com/ct/2009/mayweb-only/119-21.0.html.

10. According to ARIS, one in five adults in 2008 did not identify with a religion of any kind, compared with one in ten in 1990. See Kosmin and Keysar, "American Religious Identification Survey," ii (see n.4, above). This data also is supported by the U.S. Religious Landscape Survey, Pew Forum, 2007, religions.pewforum.org/pdf/report-religious-landscape-study-full.pdf. These statistics are also discussed in Jon Meacham's *Newsweek* cover story, "The End of Christian America," April 4, 2009, http://www.thedailybeast.com/newsweek/2009/04/03/the-end-of-christian-america.html.

11. For example, see Leonard Sweet, *Post-Modern Pilgrims: First Century Passion for the 21st Century Church* (Nashville: Broadman & Holman, 2000).

12. Diana Butler Bass, *Christianity after Religion: The End of the Church and the Birth of a New Spiritual Awakening* (New York: HarperOne, 2012), 20–26.

13. Reggie McNeal, *The Present Future: Six Tough Questions for the Church* (San Francisco: Jossey-Bass, 2003), 59.

14. David Kinnaman and Gabe Lyons, *unChristian: What a New Generation Thinks about Christianity—and Why It Matters* (Grand Rapids: Baker, 2007).

15. See "About Stillspeaking," http://www.ucc.org/god-is-still-speaking/about/.

16. Rick Warren, *The Purpose-Driven Church: Growth without Compromising Your Message and Mission* (Grand Rapids: Zondervan, 1995); idem, *The Purpose-Driven Life: What on Earth Am I Here For?* (Grand Rapids: Zondervan, 2002).

17. Jonathan Wilson, "Practicing Church: Evangelical Ecclesiologies at the End of Modernity," in *The Community of the Word: Toward an Evangelical Ecclesiology*, ed. Mark Husbands and Daniel J. Treier (Downers Grove, IL: InterVarsity Academic, 2005), 68.

18. Michael Jinkins also raises this as an appropriate question to ask of the church, for it is a question that encompasses both sides of ecclesial existence, i.e., the church's divine and human nature. See his *The Church Faces Death: Ecclesiology in a Post-Modern Context* (New York: Oxford University Press, 1999), 94.

19. Nicholas M. Healy, *Church, World, and the Christian Life: Practical-Prophetic Ecclesiology* (Cambridge: Cambridge University Press, 2000), 38.

20. Roger D. Haight, *Christian Community in History*, Vol. 1: *Historical Ecclesiology* (New York: Continuum, 2004), 19.

21. Healy, *Church, World*, 5.

22. Orthodox theologians have claimed a pneumatological focus in their ecclesiology for centuries. I borrow this phrase from D. Lyle Dabney, "Starting with the Spirit: Why the Last Should Now Be First," in *Starting with the Spirit: Task of Theology Today II*, ed. Stephen Pickard and Gordon Preece (Hindmarsh: Australian Theological Forum, 2001), 3–27. Ostensibly, such a move might also resonate with the sensibilities of the increasing number of people in the United States who describe themselves as "spiritual but not religious."

1

Ecclesiology and Context in Protestant America

When I was a pastor in Milwaukee, a parishioner gave me a book belonging to her father, who for over forty years had been the pastor of the congregation I served. The first chapter, in chronicling the history of Lutherans in Milwaukee, highlighted our congregation. What struck me, however, was the book's title: *A Plan for Survival*. A colleague who knew I was writing about the doctrine of the church quipped, "How about that for an ecclesiology!?" Despite the humorous irony, it has stuck with me, in part because it could still title an ecclesiology written today for the mainline churches.

Historically, ecclesiology has played a more peripheral role in Protestant theology (as compared to Catholic theology); however, Gregory Baum reminds us that in every period of church history, ecclesiologies emerge to address concrete problems faced by the church.[1] This chapter will consider the "questions" that the churches are asking of themselves which shape their self-understanding. Because the context for the American churches is unique, these questions must be considered against the backdrop of the relationship of the churches to the state and society. Too often, when tackling the doctrine of the church, American theologians look only to the "blueprint ecclesiologies" that were developed across the Atlantic under Christendom, including those from the Reformation tradition. The unique context of the United States specifically should be taken into account in the ecclesiological task, especially if the goal is to help actual congregations live out their identity and purpose in what Nicholas Healy calls their "ecclesiological context."[2]

In this chapter, I look at *the history of ecclesiology in America* theologically and contextually.[3] Although there are many aspects of the context that might be considered, I wish to point to one in particular: the way that the mainline churches have been culturally co-opted by a very particular form of "Christendom," the concept of a "Christian America," which has operated as a sort of a narrative that served the "modern project" in the United States.

Although the government never legally established Christianity as the national religion, as it was in Europe, there has nonetheless been a subtle, yet profound cultural establishment of Christianity, in which the goals and values of Christianity became intertwined with those of the dominant culture, in particular certain aspects of the "modern project."[4] As Douglas John Hall states, "With us in North America, Christ and culture are so inextricably connected that we hardly know where one leaves off and the other begins."[5] This chapter will trace the development of this alliance and show how it gave rise to what C. C. Goen calls the "peculiar American ecclesiology."

Before I begin this examination of American ecclesiology, let me offer a couple of caveats. First, this is not a complete survey of American ecclesiology. It focuses on certain mainline churches and their historical antecedents, because these are the churches that have been most affected by cultural Christendom—and its disestablishment—that is at the root of the current ecclesial crisis as described in the introduction. There are other Protestant denominations in the United States that have rich ecclesiological traditions, including the black churches and various Anabaptist and other Free Churches.[6] Second, because I will be discussing Lutheran contributions to ecclesiology in later chapters, it seems helpful to consider briefly the "Lutheran story" alongside the major streams of evangelical Protestantism in the United States.

VISIBLE SAINTS: THE PURITAN EXPERIMENT
IN THE SEVENTEENTH CENTURY

The Protestants who immigrated to North America brought ecclesiological ideas with them that were shaped both by their theological forebears and the context from which they came. But these ideas were further shaped by new questions and challenges that arose in the context of the new world. Since ecclesiology is always contextual, we must take into account both of these contexts.

To understand the ecclesiology of the New England Puritans, we must begin with their original ecclesial context in the Church of England. The Puritans were asking questions about the church derived from and rooted in the central ecclesiological question of the Reformation: Where can I find the *true* church? This question, along with the better-known and -covered question, "Where can I find a gracious God?," dominated Reformation theology. Paul Avis has pointed out that together these questions "constitute two aspects of the overriding concern of sixteenth-century men with the problem of salvation, for the truth of the old patristic watchword *Nulla salus extra ecclesiam*—no salvation outside the Church—was assumed on all sides."[7] John Calvin put it this way in the *Institutes:*"How necessary the knowledge of [the church] is, since there is no other means of entering into life unless she [the church] conceive us in the womb and give us birth, unless she nourish us at her breasts."[8]

Like Luther before him, Calvin held that there were two "marks" of the true church: word and sacrament.[9] Even if a church was corrupt or lacked discipline, it was still a church if it had these signs. Discipline was required for the well-being, not the existence, of the church.[10] It was not long, however, before Reformed theologians like Martin Bucer, Theodore Beza, and John Knox, as well as the leading Puritan theologians, recognized discipline as a third mark of the church. While the goal of discipline was to encourage faith and maintain Christian standards of behavior for the sake of the health of the whole church, the emphasis on discipline would shift the "question of the church" in a new direction, one that would shape Puritan thought. No longer was it enough to ask, "Where is the true (or even pure) church?" Now the question became "Who is *in* the pure church? Who are its members?"

All Puritans agreed on the need for discipline and the basic nature of the church, which early Puritan leader John Field articulated as a company of faithful people gathered from the world and set apart from the wicked.[11] According to Edmund Morgan, this conception "would have been acceptable to Puritans whether Presbyterian or Congregational, whether in England or America, whether in 1572 or 1672."[12] Because of the doctrine of election, one could never know who was "in" the invisible church. However, the Puritans became concerned to make the visible church as close an approximation of the invisible church as they possibly could. As Morgan writes, "It was too plain to the Puritans that the visible church in England stood too far from the invisible; it indiscriminately embraced the flagrantly wicked along with the good or sincerely repentant."[13] While all Puritans believed that the Church of England had become too lax in its exercise of discipline over its members, they were not of one mind as to what to do about it. The majority of Puritans believed that the "true church" still existed in the Church of England and looked to the government to help reform the church by disciplining its errant members. A small minority thought that the state church was beyond reform and that the better strategy was to "organize new churches from which the ignorant and the wicked would be excluded."[14] These Puritans came to be known as Separatists.

Even though the Separatists remained a small group (both in England and in New England), their decision nonetheless had an impact on later Puritans (including non-Separating Puritans, the majority of those who would settle New England) because they were the first to consider the ecclesiological implications of their Puritan ideals. The Separatists defended their decision to organize new churches on two grounds. First, they argued that the Church of England lacked an essential mark of the church: discipline. Puritan Henry Barrow was among those who argued that the preaching of true doctrine and the administration of the sacraments alone were not enough to make the church. Discipline also was required to enable the church to correct its own faults and for the proper administration of the sacraments, that is, in order to determine who was worthy to receive them.[15]

The second reason for separating had to do with their understanding of the church itself. Although God alone knows the members of the invisible church, for the visible church to be a proper church, it must be founded by a voluntary gathering of believers. The Separatists argued that the Church of England, as a state church, was not so founded and therefore could not be a proper church. These two points were interrelated for the Separatists: "A church must originate as a voluntary association of persons worthy to worship God. It must contain only men who freely professed to believe, and tried to live according to God's word. And it could not exist unless such men voluntarily agreed to subject themselves to discipline."[16]

Church discipline and explicit church covenants were two practical means toward achieving the purer church the Puritans desired. God elects individuals who come together voluntarily to be the church, worship God, and so forth. It is important to note here that the church covenant was not any voluntary association, but one made by the elect, which again is why the Church of England could not properly be considered a church. The covenant included both a confession and demonstrated understanding of the Christian faith, and outward behavior that reflected holy living. Certain behaviors put people clearly outside of the covenant and required their expulsion through disciplinary procedures. According to Morgan, "In the exercise of church discipline, as with the admission procedures, the Separatists concerned themselves with outward, visible behavior, and with openly expressed opinions, not with the presence or absence of saving faith."[17] It would not be until the Puritans arrived in New England that the latter would become required evidence for church membership.

Morgan argues that although it was the Separatists who laid the foundation for the distinctive Puritan ecclesiology with these ideas, it would be the immigrants who arrived a decade later, the non-Separating Puritans, who would shift the question from one of exclusion (who's out) to one of inclusion (who's in) with regard to the question of church membership. Originally, the non-Separating Puritans believed that those who were not elect "may be *in* the church, but they are not *of* it; they have fellowship in outward things, but they can have no part in effectual and saving grace."[18] Now individuals would be required to show that they possessed "saving faith" in order to become members of the church. This practice became the hallmark of radical Puritan ecclesiology.

As Calvinists, all Puritans would have agreed with Calvin that, ultimately, it is God's prerogative, not ours, to distinguish and separate the elect from the reprobate. It is a difficult task to distinguish individually who belongs to the visible church; more important is to be able to recognize where the true church is.[19] According to Calvin, those who profess the Christian faith, live the Christian life, and participate in the Christian sacraments are to be recognized as children of God. Sanctification does not, in the Protestant view, assist one in the process of salvation, although it could be a sign that one is among the elect.

As the non-Separating Puritans pointed out, however, since hypocrites and honest but unregenerate (those who are not saved) people can imitate the good works of the elect, this sign was not by itself enough to comfort doubting and weak Christians. According to Morgan, "The real problem was to find out whether one or not one had saving faith."[20] A complicated morphology of conversion was developed and preached in sermons to assist listeners in their discernment of whether or not they were among God's elect. While they were still part of the Anglican Church, they applied this idea in connection with Holy Communion since they could not apply it to membership. Once in New England the radical ramifications of this idea could be put more fully into practice. Initially, the procedures for admitting members in the first Massachusetts churches reflected those in the Plymouth church and of Separatist churches in England and Holland. Within ten years, however, such procedures came to include a test for "saving faith." John Cotton was the first major figure to make assurance of salvation dependent on an inner experience of grace, rather than on the outward signs of sanctification.[21]

Whether this was driven by the concern for a pure church or, more basically, by the need for personal assurance of salvation, the end result was a radical Puritan ecclesiology in which the distinction between the visible and invisible church was virtually collapsed.[22] The true church became the church of pure saints. The new requirement of proving that one had "saving faith" led to a shift from defining who was "out" (the visibly wicked) to now defining who was "in," those who were not only outwardly, visibly holy but those who were also able to prove they had "saving faith." The focus of ecclesiology became inward rather than outward, with an emphasis on membership, not mission. Morgan charges the Separatists and other Puritans with "ecclesiastical abdication from the world" and "virtually [denying] the evangelistic function of the church" as a result of their strict membership practices.[23] By solely focusing on gathering the saints out of the world and its sinfulness into a "pure church," the Puritans failed to recognize the church's mission to spread the gospel to others and to offer them the means of salvation. Even though, in the Calvinist schema, word and sacrament would only be effective for those who were among the elect, they were still the means through which God worked to create saving faith.

Indeed, as Morgan writes, the very life of the church was put in jeopardy; by the 1650s, few conversions had been generated and the steady migration of Puritans to the New World had ended. And worst of all, most children of the elect had not themselves received "saving faith." "As the first generation of Puritans died, the churches declined rapidly in membership and it appeared that a majority of the population would soon be unbaptized."[24] In what could be considered the first "church-growth strategy" in America, the Puritans in New England developed what came to be known (somewhat derisively) as the "Halfway Covenant." This stipulated that those who did not receive "saving faith" could still receive some of the benefits of membership as long as they professed the doctrines of the Christian faith and lived a life free of scandal. They could receive the discipline of the church and could have their children baptized, but they could not vote or receive communion. According to Morgan, the Halfway Covenant was an attempt to answer questions created by the rigorous concept of membership and its negative effects on the church population. It reflected not, as is often thought, a decline in piety but "an honest attempt to rescue the concept of a church of visible saints from the tangle of problems created in time by human reproduction."[25]

The Puritan concept of covenant and its radical ecclesiology would provide the basis for the Puritan understanding of a "Christian America." The Puritans arrived in the colonies with the hope of establishing a Christian society based on biblical laws and spoke of America's election through the covenant and role in God's providence. As Perry Miller notes, "When the Puritans came to New England the idea had not yet dawned that a government could safely permit several creeds to exist side by side within the confines of a single nation."[26] Indeed, "to allow no dissent from the truth was exactly the reason why they had come to America."[27] John Winthrop's 1645 speech on liberty is the classic articulation of this Puritan goal. "As [Winthrop] expounds it, the political doctrine becomes part and parcel of the theological, and the cord that binds all ideas together is the covenant."[28] It is only those who become regenerate through the covenant of grace who are at liberty to do what God commands and enact God's covenant with the government. From its inception, the Massachusetts Bay Colony sought "to prove that the Bible could be made a rule of life, that essentials of religion could be derived from Scripture, and then reinforced by the enlightened dictation of godly magistrates."[29] The Puritan understanding of the function of the state reflected the legacy of Christendom in that they believed that "government was established by God to save depraved men from their own depravity."[30] The idea of a "holy society" was built on the notion that the regenerate could of their own free will and choice make decisions that would reflect God's will in the commonwealth.

The social theory of the Puritans had as its foundation the exclusionary Puritan ecclesiology discussed above. As Miller notes, "The congregational system, with its membership limited to those who had proved before the church that they possessed the signs of grace, offered a ready machinery for winnowing the wheat from the chaff."[31] God established a covenant with the regenerate not only for the sake of their salvation, but for the sake of the commonwealth. Not only the ability to hold elected office, but even the right to vote in civic society, was limited to those who could demonstrate that they were among the elect. Miller points out the difficulty of this system in light of the fact that the unregenerate outnumbered the regenerate five to one. "In New England, the unregenerate were an ever-present reality. The majority of the populace were expected to live quietly under a church system which not only held them without the pale, but insinuated that they were in all probability damned."[32]

Miller contends that it was the ultimate failure of the Puritan experiment to establish a pure church and a holy society—and not just the increasing plurality of Christian groups in the colonies—that led to a new basis for governance, one that eventually would be reflected in the founding documents of the United States. He writes, "The divine ordinance and the spirit of God, which were supposed to have presided over the political process, vanished, leaving a government founded on the self-evident truths of the law of nature, brought into being by social compact, instituted not for the glory of God, but to secure men's 'inalienable rights' of life, liberty, and the pursuit of happiness."[33] This does not mean that later Americans would not see the hand of God in the progress of their new country. Indeed, as Sacvan Bercovitch has shown, the foundation for a progressive view of history was first laid by the Puritans, who joined together two understandings of providence into one figural symbol, *Americanus*. While the Puritans spoke primarily of the providence of the human soul, they also applied this concept to groups of people. These were further separated into two types: *secular providences*, which apply to all people, such as God's providential care of all people by sending rain; and *figural providences*, God's acts of mercy and privilege that extend only to the elect people, "the subjects of ecclesiastical history from Abraham through David and Nehemiah to Winthrop."[34] In making Jonathan Winthrop the "representative American," Cotton Mather (1663–1728), the grandson of John Cotton, conflated these two kinds of providences, whereby God's providence is worked out in America not only in terms of the redemption of individuals, but also the redeemer nation. In this way, Mather provided "a ready framework for inverting later secular values—human perfectibility, technological progress, democracy, Christian socialism, or simply (and comprehensively) the American Way—into the model of sacred teleology."[35]

From Visible Saints to Voluntary Society and the Narrative of "Christian America"

The Puritan idea of a holy society, wherein God's covenant with society was based on God's covenant with the church, would fail in large part due to its own inherent difficulties. The Puritan concern for the true church and the related anxiety regarding membership in the true church would give way to new theological questions, in spite of the fact that many new groups of immigrants (including many German Lutherans) continued to arrive, asking different versions of this same question. By the end of the eighteenth century, with the advent of the free exercise of religion as established by the U.S. Constitution (and eventually by every state), these groups established their particular ecclesial identities while at the same time learning to live alongside of other churches. By the mid-nineteenth century, various streams of thought from the American Enlightenment and nineteenth-century revivalism converged to create what I call the narrative of a Christian America. This also shapes the question of the church. While the Puritans laid the groundwork for the narrative of a Christian America, the end of the Puritan Commonwealth[36] left the narrative in need of a new foundation: the church as voluntary association.

Although the voluntary principle had roots in the Puritan experience (wherein members joined together voluntarily versus compulsorily, that is, by state law), it was reinterpreted by these new streams of thought. Its application would go beyond church membership and its concern with individual salvation; it came to be employed to assist churches in living together under the First

Amendment. But, even more significantly, the voluntary principle enabled churches to work together toward even larger goals. Whereas in the Puritan schema it was the government's role first and foremost to protect the church and the truth of the gospel, the churches—by means of voluntary cooperation—would now support the progress of a virtuous republic. The question of the "true church" and its concern for membership gave way to questions about how the churches could participate in transforming society into the kingdom of God—increasingly understood as the progress of a nation. By the nineteenth century, the covenant language of the Puritans began to be applied directly to American civilization.[37] The question shifted from one of membership to one of purpose and unity: How are Christians able to work together for the promulgation of the kingdom of God as seen in the progress of a "Christian America"?

THE AMERICAN ENLIGHTENMENT AND THE MODERN PROJECT IN THE EIGHTEENTH CENTURY

It is important to first make a distinction between "modern project" and the "modern period," since the word *modernity* is used interchangeably for both.[38] The modern period began at the end of the eighteenth century and was marked by two major events: the Industrial Revolution and the democratic revolution. The transition to the modern period coincided with the emergence of a new understanding of reason that enabled Enlightenment thinkers "to develop objective science, universal morality and law, and autonomous art according to their inner logic."[39] The modern project used the "objective science" of rational analysis in order to gain new knowledge and technology for the twin goals of progress and emancipation. In short, the right use of reason led to advances in all arenas of human life: improved health and overall human welfare, educational systems, increased economic production and creation of wealth, and wider social and economic opportunities for a greater number of people through democratic governance.

The relationship of the churches to the Enlightenment and the modern project is more complex than is often thought. While many American Protestants rejected certain aspects of the Enlightenment, these same Christians readily endorsed the moral and social ideals and attitudes of the emerging modern age, especially ideas like progress, commerce, and individualism.[40] In his magisterial study of the Enlightenment in America, Henry May outlines four major (often overlapping) forms of the Enlightenment in Europe that were imported to and had an impact on American thought.[41]

The *first* form of the Enlightenment to take root in American soil was the "Moderate or Rational Enlightenment" (1688–1787). This form dominated England from the time of Newton and Locke until the mid-eighteenth century and held to the "reasonableness of Christianity," which reconciled Newtonian science with Christian miracles and stressed order, balance, moderation, and religious compromise. The First Great Awakening (1739–1740), with its emphasis on the "religion of the heart," sought to point out the limits of natural religion and to reassert in its place central tenets of Calvinism such as divine sovereignty and human dependence.[42] The ideas of the Moderate Enlightenment were also challenged by a *second* form, "The Skeptical Enlightenment" (1750–1789), led by Voltaire, but unsurprisingly, this form would find the least support in the colonies, especially among the clergy.

The *third* form, the "Revolutionary Enlightenment" (1776–1800), opposed both English moderation and French skepticism. It culminated in the thought of Thomas Paine whose pamphlet *Common Sense* "is full of the excitement of a moment when men have a chance to form their institutions anew."[43] Many of the ideas of the Revolutionary Enlightenment—including the break from the English monarchy and tradition, and the establishment of religious liberty—were initially supported by the majority of moderate and ultra-Calvinists, radical Separatists, Arminians, and Deists alike. Nevertheless, the excesses of the French Revolution and the Jacobins led other clergy to lump Voltaire, Paine, and Thomas Jefferson together, and to see them all "as heirs of a conspiracy of philosophers against all religious and social order."[44]

With Jefferson's presidential election in 1800 and the emergence of two growing churches that were solidly Jeffersonian—the Baptists and Methodists—the anti-Jacobin, Calvinist rhetoric of the New England clergy gave way to that of the revival. This shift had drastic implications for American religion and culture. Most significantly, it effectively ended the theological stronghold of Calvinism and reshaped American religion in the nineteenth century into a popular evangelicalism that was "flexible, activist, moralistic, [and] increasingly un-theological."[45] Many of the Federalist clergy also began transferring their energies from anti-Jacobin crusades into missionary activity and social reform, defeating what remained of the Skeptical and Revolutionary phases of the American Enlightenment.

And yet, the values of the Moderate Enlightenment were too deeply embedded in American government and its founding documents for the Enlightenment to be completely rejected. A new basis was needed upon which rationality, progress, and morality could be articulated and defended. This brings us to May's *fourth* form of the Enlightenment in America, the "Didactic

Enlightenment" (1800–1815). Based on Scottish Common Sense philosophy, this form became the principal mode in which the Enlightenment was assimilated into the formative period of nineteenth-century American culture. Its three main tenets were: "the essential reality and dependability of moral values, the certainty of progress, and the usefulness and importance of 'culture' in the narrower sense, especially literature."[46] In particular, the second of these tenets—the certainty of progress—became central to the emerging narrative of a Christian America.

THE CENTRALITY AND CERTAINTY OF PROGRESS IN THE NINETEENTH CENTURY

Various bursts of growth experienced by the new nation, beginning in 1815, propelled the idea of progress.[47] With the end of the War of 1812 and the fall of Napoleon, the new republic seemed assured of its independence, economic prosperity, and a continually expanding frontier. The movement westward, combined with the growth of the nation's natural resources, led to a tremendous boom in the population. These were also the decades of the Industrial Revolution and invention of new technologies (1790–1890) and the building of the first transcontinental railroad (completed in 1869), all of which contributed to the increasing economic prosperity America was experiencing. "With concrete evidences of material advancement on every side, progress was the faith of the common man as well as of the philosopher," writes Arthur Ekirch. The "faith in progress" was not limited to material advances, but came to be extended to intellectual and moral improvements as democracy began to flourish on the state level, and as a public-school system was established to educate the population.[48]

According to Stow Persons, a fusion of three ideological streams of thought at the end of the nineteenth century formed the "intellectual matrix of the modern age."[49] These were (1) the voluntary principle, (2) democratic social ideology, and (3) naturalistic ideas, especially positivism and evolutionary theory. It is this third stream of thought that represented the sharpest and most dramatic departure from established religious traditions in the history of intellectual thought. The theologian was challenged to find ways to speak of Christian truths in light of new scientific theories. As Persons notes, however, "the most significant consequence of evolutionism for intellectual history was *not* the recasting of traditional and conventional conceptions of the ultimate origins of life or the universe," but the way evolutionary theory shaped a worldview as seen from the perspective of the present, an interpretation of history itself as morally, spiritually, and intellectually progressive.[50] This progressive view of history became a key tenet in the development of liberal Protestant theology, in both its evangelical and modernist forms, at the end of the nineteenth and beginning of the twentieth century.

THE VOLUNTARY PRINCIPLE

As noted above, the Puritan experiment of a Christian commonwealth failed for many reasons. However, the idea of sustaining a Christian society was so deeply rooted in the culture that it could not be abandoned. Instead, it was given a new foundation in this period: the voluntary principle. The voluntary principle in religion is a broad concept that actually incorporates two distinct ideas: (1) the church itself as a voluntary association of believers and (2) the free cooperation of congregations, denominations, and individuals for common causes in promotion of a virtuous republic (such as social reform, church revitalization, missions, antislavery, and prohibition).[51] The methods of these free associations were persuasive, not coercive. The voluntary principle was, at the same time, one of the influences that contributed to the victory of religious liberty in America and a means for churches not only to survive, but also thrive in a situation where churches were no longer under state control.

While it worked well in many regards, it also began to shape a distinctive "American ecclesiology" whereby the church was defined not only structurally (as distinct from the state church), but also more anthropologically (rather than theologically). C. C. Goen argues that the voluntary principle made this anthropological foundation inevitable for the church, going so far as to say that the American churches' accommodation to American culture has been a "loss of the doctrine of the church itself."[52] The church came to be viewed as a society that existed on the basis of human will and cooperation. Further, because membership was defined less by doctrinal beliefs and more by common purpose, the concept of the church as voluntary association tended to "push tangible, practical considerations to the fore by placing primary emphasis on the free, uncoerced consent of the individual."[53] Sidney Mead further states that this led to Christianity being conceived primarily as an activity or movement that the group was engaged in promoting.[54] The voluntary principle itself allowed for the churches' self-understanding to be shaped by the narrative of a "Christian America."[55]

Thus the nineteenth century opened with the goal of maintaining the Christian character of the nation by voluntary means. In the first half of the nineteenth century, the same arguments for morality and order that had been used to support colonial religious establishments now were used to advocate for the Christianization of society by methods of persuasion.[56] As Robert Handy shows, however, the vision of a Christian America that was gained by voluntary means subtly changed in a critical way over the course of the nineteenth century. Earlier in the century, the priority of the religious vision was strongly and widely maintained; it was Christianity and civilization, Christianity as the best part of civilization, and its hope. In the latter part of the century [1860–1890], however, in most cases unconsciously, much of the real focus had shifted to the civilization itself, with Christianity and the churches finding their significance in relation to it. Civilization itself was given increasingly positive assessment, chiefly because it was understood to have absorbed much of the spirit of Christianity.[57]

Clergy such as Samuel Harris (1814–1899) posited that modern ideas, such as the promise of human progress, civil rights, the rule of justice and love, the elimination of oppression, and the "brotherhood of man and the Fatherhood of God," are all derived from the gospel, so much so that "the mission of Christian faith was virtually being identified with national destiny, with the progress of civilization."[58] Religious leaders began to interpret advances in democratic reforms, progress in science and technology, and the growth of industrialization as fruits of the increasing civilization of society and a sign of the coming of Christ's kingdom.[59] "'A grand feature of our times is that *all* is *Progress*,' exulted the editors of *The Independent* in 1851," writes Timothy Smith. "Christianity and culture seemed to be marching together 'onward and upward' toward the 'grant consummation of prophecy in a civilized, an enlightened, and a sanctified world' and the establishment of 'that spiritual kingdom which God has ordained shall triumph and endure.'"[60]

REVIVALISM AND THE KINGDOM OF GOD

How and why did these Protestant leaders come to understand these advances as signs of the kingdom of God? The Puritan concept of providence offered the ready framework for inverting "the American way" into the model of sacred teleology, so that by the mid-nineteenth century the progress of a nation came to be interpreted as signifying the coming kingdom of God. But it was the emerging new revivalism that would solidify this way of thinking. By the mid-nineteenth century, revivalism was "adopted and promoted in one form or another by major segments of all denominations."[61] Significantly, these nineteenth-century revival measures "went hand in hand with progressive theology and humanitarian concerns."[62]

Although they were relative newcomers to American Protestantism at the turn of the nineteenth century, Baptists and Methodists had become dominant by 1855, comprising 70 percent of the total number of communing Protestants. With the emergence of these groups came also the theological dominance of Arminianism and its doctrine of free will that opened the promise—and hope—of salvation universally to all people, not only those who had been predestined for salvation. "To the hopeful concepts of free will and a universal atonement," Smith notes, "Methodism added the promise of man's immediate perfectibility, not by reason or education, but through the operation of the spirit of God."[63] The popularity of this idea increased steadily from 1840 to 1870. The focus of the doctrine of Christian perfection was the personal holiness of the individual, but Christians would soon embrace the possibilities of this doctrine for addressing various social ills as well. Thus from the fires of revival Christianity emerged "a platform more widely acceptable and as realistically concerned with alleviating social evil. It called for the miraculous baptism of believers in the Holy Ghost and the consecration of their lives and possessions to the building of the kingdom of God."[64] Led by the Holy Spirit and millenialist fervor, the regenerate saw that it was their task not only to preach the gospel to all people, but also to transform society in accordance with God's will.

In contrast to the inward-looking Puritans, who were more concerned with who was in and who was out, these outward-looking evangelicals were concerned with putting their salvation to work by transforming society into the kingdom of God. Indeed, Smith contends that the rapid pace at which churches concerned themselves with social issues such as poverty, worker's rights, liquor sales, slum housing conditions, and racial tensions "is the chief feature distinguishing American religion after 1865 from that of the first half of the nineteenth century."[65] One of the fruits of this shift in focus was that ethical concerns would be stressed more than dogmatic ones in the preaching and teaching ministry of the church.

These changes were accompanied by two other significant changes that were outgrowths of the broader application of the voluntary principle: an expansion of lay participation and control in the ministry of the church and the maturing of a "spirit of interdenominational brotherhood" that many of the leading clergymen promoted.[66] Pastors began to speak of the present division of Christians as sinful. According to Smith, although the spirit of unity between Christian denominations had been growing for many years, it was the absence of "sectarian bigotry" that distinguished the mid-nineteenth-century revivals from previous ones.

The narrative of a progressive Christian America was at its height in this period—paradoxically, as the nation finally faced the evils of slavery and found itself embroiled in the Civil War. The voluntary principle would help to shape an ecclesiology that would become increasingly sociological and pragmatic, as Goen notes. Individual believers voluntarily assembled in order to serve a greater good, in this case, the promulgation of God's kingdom through a Christian nation. Theological reflection on the doctrine of the church in this period was limited, except for pragmatic concerns for Christian unity in service of the larger goal of social transformation. The peculiar American ecclesiology—a sociological concept of the church based in the voluntary principle—would serve the needs of church members and the goals of "Christian America" well for several more decades. It was not until the twentieth century that ecclesiology proper began to receive attention by mainline Protestants—but then only by ecumenists; the *de facto* ecclesiology for these mainline Protestant churches remained the "voluntary association." This concept was further bolstered in the early twentieth century by the growth of the denomination as the means of church organization and structure and the kind of institutional concerns brought about by this structural change. Goen states the negative legacy of this concept in stark terms: "Three centuries ago the question, 'What is the church?' was of crucial, even revolutionary importance. Today it is diffidently asked, rarely answered, and indeed scarcely visible—having been displaced by more urgent questions about growth, efficiency, dollars."[67]

THE "LUTHERAN DIFFERENCE"?

Before considering how the shift to a de facto "post-Christendom" offer a new perspective on this narrative—and the role and identity of the churches in it—I would like to briefly consider the place of Lutheranism in the exposition of a "Christian America." In many ways, because of their particular confessional and cultural heritage, Lutherans have operated more as "outsiders" to this narrative, possessing the "Lutheran difference."[68] As an immigrant church that gained its largest growth in membership through emigration from Germany and Scandinavian countries in the mid- to late nineteenth century, Lutherans historically found themselves culturally outside of the mainstream of American Protestantism. This was due both to language and cultural differences these immigrants brought as well as to their distinctive confessional tradition. While there are many points of connection between Lutheranism and other Protestant traditions, including an understanding of the church as "created" by the word (a concept we will return to in the next chapter), the Lutheran theological heritage is distinct in several ways from Calvinism and Arminianism.

Lutherans were among those in the nineteenth century who rejected or severely criticized the voluntary principle as a basis for ecclesiological understanding.[69] For all the differences between different Lutheran immigrant groups, nearly all Lutherans in the nineteenth century—whether confessional German or pietistic Norwegian Lutherans—rejected the notion that the church is gathered and unified by the will of people with a common purpose. Lutherans as a whole were also wary of revivalism, which was closely bound up with voluntarism. At the same time, however, thanks in large part to the work of William A. Passavant, Lutherans did adopt voluntarism on a larger scale, developing many associations for the betterment of society that had pan-Lutheran support. Passavant, who "wanted his church to be an aggressive force in America, to be a working as well as a worshipping and witnessing community," established four hospitals and several orphanages, and introduced deaconess work.[70]

One also needs to be clear in defining "Americanization." While for most Lutherans the question of Americanization has been focused primarily on the mid-nineteenth-century debate over sacramental theology, its broader influence on Lutherans has not been as readily recognized. While immigrants who arrived in the second half of the nineteenth century did reflect more "old world" concerns, particularly regarding their ecclesial identity over and against state church practices, they were not so ghettoized as not to be ultimately affected by larger social, political, and cultural trends of "Americanization." As these Lutherans joined the mainstream of Protestant evangelicalism—sociologically, if not theologically—they began to be shaped by the narrative of a Christian America. In fact, E. Clifford Nelson argues that by standing against all forms of culture-religion, Lutherans mis-interpreted, or at least gave one-sided emphasis to, a facet of Lutheran theology, and they did not escape captivity to culture-religion by minimizing the public and prophetic role of the church. As a matter of fact, Lutheran congregations across the land in the prosperous fifties gave evidence that they were enamored of the desire for popular approval and success. Accepting uncritically the approbation of middle-class America, Lutheranism was in danger of becoming what its theology did not allow, a culture-religion.[71]

Further, even if the Lutherans—or any other immigrant minority denominations—have not consciously defined their ecclesial understanding by this narrative, the argument could be made that the unchurched do not make the theological distinctions that churchgoers do. From the outside, so to speak, this narrative applies to all the Protestant churches. The context demands that all of the mainline Protestant churches recognize the power that this narrative has had in shaping a peculiarly American ecclesiology.

THE DISESTABLISHMENT OF THE CHURCHES

In spite of the fact that progress and providence had become one concept in the minds of many Christian Americans, the realities of postwar life spiritual and economic recession, and a decrease in crusading zeal, led to the erosion of the quest for a Protestant America in the 1920s.[72] While Christianity had certainly influenced civilization, some church leaders began to worry that that influence could go both ways. Handy writes, "The religion also became so attached to the civilization that as the latter changed it was difficult for many Protestants to sense to what degree they had become a religion of the culture." By the mid-1930s, however, several Protestant leaders feared that rather than Christianizing society, civilization had "captured the church."[73]

Handy decries this period as the "end of the Protestant Era," but it would not be the death of this narrative. Even as the Second World War raised questions and challenges to the concept of progress, it also brought a new revival of religion, fused with nationalistic impulses. Martin Marty has suggested that in the wake of this development, the new shape emerging in American religion was not so much a "revival of historic Christianity as it was a revival of interest in 'religion-in-general.' More specifically, it was a 'religion of democracy' that emerged as America's real religion, in part a sociological replacement of the old dream of a Christian America."[74] Robert Bellah gave this phenomenon the commonly accepted coinage of "American Civil Religion."[75] The experience of World War II was cast in terms of a fight for democracy and freedom, and civil religion gave new impetus and articulation to America's special role in providence, as a nation under God's law called to carry out God's will on earth, particularly by sharing the "light" of democracy with other nations. America's leadership in technological advances during this period also added to the narrative of progress. Bellah is careful to state that civil religion is not the worship of the American nation but, rather, is "at best a genuine apprehension of universal and transcendent religious reality as seen in or, one could almost say, as revealed through the experience of the American people."[76] Douglas John Hall's concern is less with the idea of civil religion itself and more with its influence on the churches, which has resulted in the overshadowing of the church's unique mission and message by that of the nation and a loss of a theological identity of the church.

As Hall and others have also pointed out, however, the final vestiges of "cultural Christianity"—in the form of an American civil religion—have been undergoing a process of "disestablishment" since the 1960s "with the collapse or substantial erosion of much of the churched culture that had been built up over a period of two hundred years."[77] As the narrative of a Christian America breaks down, the church's place in the narrative is also being questioned. More and more people are not looking to the church as the "means of salvation" (visible saints) nor as the means to improve society (voluntary association), although the intermittent resurgence of the Religious Right since the 1980s would suggest that the latter is still alive and well in many respects. With increased attention to personal freedom and rights in many arenas, "notions of shared public morals gave way to personal decisions of expediency, pleasure, or private judgment. . . . People no longer assumed that the church had anything relevant to say on matters beyond personal faith. Public policy became increasingly secularized, as public morals became increasingly personalized and privatized."[78]

Thus the church finds itself in "the awkwardly intermediate stage of having once been culturally established but . . . not yet clearly disestablished."[79] On the one hand, "the churches have become so accommodated to the American way of life that they are now domesticated, and it is no longer obvious what justifies their existence as particular communities."[80] On the other hand, the church has been dislodged from its particular role as a chaplain to the culture, and the privilege, influence, and public voice that went along with that position. Indeed, not only has the church lost its public voice, it no longer seems to have any hegemony with regard to the "private" side of religion either, with the concurrent growing religious pluralism in the United States.[81]

How Shall the Church Respond?

According to Hall, the most common response has been to recognize that things are not what they were, but to go on behaving as if nothing has changed.[82] Increasingly, with the precipitous decline in church membership, this has become less and less of an option for the mainline congregations. The crisis of "mainline decline" has agitated churches to address this crisis, usually by asking, "What can we do to grow again? How can we turn this trend around?" The solutions assume a voluntary concept of the church, are pragmatic, and focus on strategies to reverse the decline in membership and return to the "golden days" of church activity. For most mainline Protestants, this means a return to the post–World War II era, when the sanctuaries and Sunday school classrooms were full and the church had a clear role as "chaplain" to the nation, blessing America and its values of freedom, progress, and democracy, all the while blissfully denying the cost to humanity and creation.[83] In addition to adapting the voluntary principle to entrepreneurial ends, others have sought to form new alliances in an attempt to regain a position of political and cultural influence.[84] Indeed, Hall notes with irony that the very failure of the New World Dream has in some sense enhanced the public role of religion. For large numbers of our fellow citizens are unable to face the decline of their culture, and many look to the churches to help them repress their social doubt and identity crisis. . . . Now these churches are expected to reinforce the social vision of success long after it has ceased concretely to inform most other institutions of the society, even government. Now one goes to church in order to be able to believe in America again.[85]

In both cases, most of us are still "'dreaming Christendom dreams.' We envy the seeming success of the Christian Right, and we are made respondent by our reductions."[86] As I argued in the introduction, none of these solutions get to the heart of the ecclesial crisis, which is first and foremost a crisis of *identity*. We do not know "who we are" as "church" anymore, in part because we have allowed our purpose to be shaped by the narrative of a Christian America and because most of us are operating in practice with the concept of the church as a voluntary association. At its worst, the voluntary principle has led to a view of the church in which the needs of the individual and the institution become of primary concern, and not God. Michael Horton agrees: "Taken to its extreme, [such] thinking easily leads to the view expressed by George Barna, an evangelical pioneer of church marketing: 'Think of your church not as a religious meeting place, but as a service agency—an entity that exists to satisfy people's needs.'"[87] The language of marketing has found its way into the imaginations of most churchgoers these days as congregations wrestle with declining attendance. Individuals go "church shopping" for congregations that will meet their needs. People choose churches because they are seeking something for themselves: a spiritual journey, fellowship, peace and comfort in times of difficulty, or even the need to make a difference in the world.

As Reggie McNeal and others have pointed out, churches are still operating as if the majority of people are looking to have these needs met in Christian congregations. The church must come to grips with the changing context in which its identity and role are no longer presumed in the same way. In other words, people are turning to other resources to meet these needs. Perhaps even more importantly, while these are not wrong reasons to join a congregation, they are not enough by themselves. We are the church not because of anything we decide or need (or even what society needs), including our desire that our congregations survive in this time of "mainline decline." The argument of this book is that we are the church because of what *God* has decided and is doing for our redemption—and because of what *God* desires for the sake of God's mission in the world.

As long as we continue to operate with this concept as the *de facto* American ecclesiology and its corresponding focus on meeting individual needs, we will keep asking the wrong questions and coming up with the wrong solutions to the challenges facing the churches. What is needed is a robustly theological concept of the church that begins with *who God is* and *what God is doing.*

For Reflection and Discussion

1. How did the non-Separating Puritans lay the foundation for radical Puritan ecclesiology, according to Edmund Morgan? What did this lead them to deny?

2. The ecclesiology of the Puritans was driven by questions related to the "true church" and belonging to the true church. Do you see these concerns reflected in mainline Protestant churches today? In what way?

3. How do the ecclesial ideas of the Puritans provide a basis for the narrative of a "Christian America?" How have the mainline churches both influenced and been influenced by this narrative? Can you think of specific examples in your own congregation?

4. What does it mean to think of the church as a "voluntary association?" What are the positive and negative legacies of this idea? How do you see this concept shaping the ecclesiological views of church members today?

5. What shifts in ecclesiology occur in the mid-nineteenth century with the emergence of the new revivalism?

6. How have you seen what Douglas John Hall calls the "disestablishment" of the churches in your lifetime? How have congregations you know responded to this new reality? Are they still "dreaming Christendom dreams"? How do you think they *should* they respond?

Notes

1. Gregory Baum, "The Church in a North-American Perspective," in Gerard Mannion and Lewis S. Mudge, eds., *Routledge Companion to Ecclesiology* (New York: Routledge, 2008), 331.

2. Nicolas M. Healy, *Church, World, and the Christian Life: Practical-Prophetic Ecclesiology* (Cambridge: Cambridge University Press, 2000), 38.

3. While there have been many studies of the ecclesiologies of individual denominations, movements, and individuals in the United States, few have attempted a historical survey of ecclesiological thinking in North America or even the United States. For such an attempt from a sociological perspective, see Baum, "Church," 326–41.

4. Douglas John Hall, *The Reality of the Gospel and the Unreality of the Churches* (Philadelphia: Westminster, 1975), 103–104.

5. Douglas John Hall, *The End of Christendom and the Future of Christianity,* Christian Mission and Modern Culture (Valley Forge: Trinity Press International, 1997), 29.

6. It is not that these traditions are not worth consideration in a discussion of ecclesiology. In fact, the Anabaptist tradition is seen by some theologians (such as John Howard Yoder) to offer a helpful alternative concept of the church to the culturally captivated of the mainline churches, of the church as "counterculture."

7. Paul D. L. Avis, *The Church in the Theology of the Reformers* (Atlanta: John Knox, 1981), 1.

8. John T. McNeill, ed., *Calvin: Institutes of the Christian Faith*, trans. and indexed by Ford Lewis Battles, Library of Christian Classics, vol. 21 (Philadelphia: Westminster, 1960), 2283 [Bk. 4, Ch. 1, Sect. 4].

9. Calvin wrote, "Wherever we see the Word of God sincerely preached and heard; wherever we see the sacraments administered according to the institution of Christ: there we cannot have any doubt that the Church of God has some existence." Ibid., 2289 [Bk. 4, Ch. 1, Sect. 9].

10. Ibid., 2453 [Bk. 4, Ch. 12, Sect. 1].

11. Cited in Edmund S. Morgan, *Visible Saints: The History of a Puritan Idea* (Ithaca: Cornell University Press, 1965), 14.

12. Ibid.

13. Ibid., 10.

14. Ibid., 16.

15. Ibid., 23.

16. Ibid., 25

17. Ibid., 47.

18. Perry Miller, *Orthodoxy in Massachusetts 1630–1650s: A Genetic Study* (Cambridge: Harvard University Press, 1933), 54–55 (italics mine).

19. David N. Wiley, "The Church as the Elect in the Theology of John Calvin," in *John Calvin and the Church* (Louisville: Westminster John Knox, 1990), 101.

20. Morgan, *Visible Saints*, 67.

21. Stephen Brachlow, *Communion of Saints: Radical Puritan and Separatist Ecclesiology, 1570–1625* (New York: Oxford University Press, 1988), 133.

22. Ibid., 115.

23. Morgan, *Visible Saints*, 117, 120.

24. Ibid., 129.

25. Ibid., 137.

26. Perry Miller, *Errand into the Wilderness* (Cambridge: Belknap Press of Harvard University Press, 1956), 144.

27. Ibid., 145.

28. Ibid., 148.

29. Miller, *Orthodoxy*, 50.

30. Miller, *Errand*, 144.

31. Ibid., 150.

32. Miller, *Orthodoxy*, 206–207.

33. Miller, *Errand*, 151.

34. Sacvan Bercovitch, *The Puritan Origins of the American Self* (New Haven: Yale University Press, 1975), 41.

35. Ibid., 136.

36. The Puritan Commonwealth officially came to an end when it lost its colonial charter in 1684, but other scholars argue that it was the Salem Witch trials in 1692 which really ended the experiment. Still others argue that the history of the Puritan Commonwealth lingered on until the First Great Awakening in 1739–40. See George McKenna, *The Puritan Origins of American Patriotism* (New Haven: Yale University Press, 2009), 2–3.

37. Timothy L. Smith, *Revivalism and Social Reform: American Protestantism on the Eve of the Civil War* (New York: Harper & Row, 1957), 156.

38. This distinction is made by Jürgen Habermas in "Modernity: An Incomplete Project," in *The Anti-Aesthetic: Essays on Postmodern Culture*, ed. Hal Foster (Port Townsend, WA: Bay Press, 1983), 9.

39. Ibid.

40. Sidney Mead, *The Lively Experiment: The Shaping of Christianity in America* (New York: Harper & Row, 1963), 127.

41. Henry F. May, *The Enlightenment in America* (New York: Oxford University Press, 1976). May's own definition of the Enlightenment is broad. It includes "all those who believe two propositions: first, that the present age is more enlightened than the past; and second, that we understand nature and man best through the use of our natural faculties," thereby excluding "all . . . who think that the surest guide for human beings is revelation, tradition or illumination" (xiv).

42. Ibid., 42–43.

43. Ibid., 162.

44. Ibid., 252.

45. Ibid., 324.

46. Ibid., 358.

47. For the following, see Arthur A. Ekirch, *The Idea of Progress in America, 1815–1860* (New York: Peter Smith, 1951), 34–37.

48. Ibid., 36–37.

49. Stow Persons, "Religion and Modernity, 1865–1914," in *The Shaping of American Religion*, vol. 1: *Religion in American Life*, ed. James W. Smith and A. Leland Jamison (Princeton: Princeton University Press, 1961), 370.

50. Ibid., 378, my emphasis.

51. See James Luther Adams, "The Voluntary Principle," in *The Religion of the Republic*, ed. Elwyn Smith (Philadelphia: Fortress Press, 1971), 217–46.

52. See C. C. Goen, "Ecclesiocracy without Ecclesiology: Denominational Life in America," *Religion in Life* 48 (1979): 17–31.

53. Mead, *Lively Experiment*, 113.

54. Ibid., 114.

55. This church concept is not the same thing as "free-church ecclesiology," although the voluntary principle is perhaps even more easily adapted by churches with such polity. A free-church polity describes not only freedom from state establishment, but freedom from any structures beyond the congregation. That is why I do not include free-church ecclesiology as a significant component in the development of the concept of the church as "voluntary association." Most of the mainline churches in the United States (the major exception being the Congregationalists) did not have free-church polities, as they had some sort connective structure beyond the congregation itself (whether the presbytery, the synod, or the episcopacy).

56. Robert T. Handy, *A Christian America: Protestant Hopes and Historical Realities* (New York: Oxford University Press, 1971), 36. See also Elwyn A. Smith, "The Voluntary Establishment of Religion," in *The Religion of the Republic*, 155.

57. Handy, *Christian America*, 110.

58. Ibid., 110, 111.

59. Ibid., 121.

60. Smith, *Revivalism and Social Reform*, 226.

61. Ibid., 45.

62. Smith, *Revivalism and Social Reform*, 60.

63. Ibid., 15, 25.

64. Ibid., 146.

65. Ibid., 148.

66. Ibid., 80.

67. Goen, "Ecclesiocracy," 29.

68. The phrase is Mark A. Noll's, in "The Lutheran Difference," *First Things* 20 (April 1992): 31–40.

69. Adams, "Voluntary Principle," 239.

70. E. Clifford Nelson, *The Lutherans in North America*, rev. ed. (Philadelphia: Fortress Press, 1980), 299.

71. Ibid., 525–26.

72. Handy, *Christian America*, 206.

73. Ibid., 210–11.

74. Marty is cited in ibid., 220. See also Mead, *The Nation with the Soul of a Church* (New York: Harper & Row, 1975), 12–18.

75. Robert N. Bellah, "Civil Religion in America," and "American Civil Religion in the 1970s," in *American Civil Religion*, ed. Russell E. Richey and Donald G. Jones (New York: Harper & Row, 1974), 21–44; 255–72.

76. Bellah, "Civil Religion in America," 33.

77. Darrell Guder, ed., *Missional Church: A Vision for the Sending of the Church in North America*, The Gospel and Our Culture (Grand Rapids: Eerdmans, 1998), 54. This book was authored by a team of theologians; the primary drafter of this chapter was Craig Van Gelder.

78. Ibid.

79. George Lindbeck, *The Nature of Doctrine: Religion and Theology in a Postliberal Age* (Philadelphia: Westminster, 1984), 134, cited by Hall in "Ecclesia Crucis: The Disciple Community and the Future of the Church in North America," *Union Seminary Quarterly Review* 46, nos. 1–4 (1992): 59.

80. Guder, ed., *Missional Church,* 78. The primary drafter of this chapter was George Hunsburger.

81. This is another fruit of the voluntary principle. See Wade Clark Roof, "America's Voluntary Establishment: Mainline Religion in Transition," in *Religion and America: Spiritual Life in a Secular Age*, ed. Mary Douglas and Steven Tipton (Boston: Beacon, 1982), 130–49.

82. See Douglas John Hall's discussion in *The Future of the Church: Where Are We Headed?* (Toronto: United Church Pub. House, 1989).

83. See the discussion in Rodney Clapp, *Johnny Cash and the Great American Contradiction: Christianity and the Battle for the Soul of a Nation* (Louisville: Westminster John Knox, 2008), 63–80.

84. Michael Jinkins, *The Church Faces Death: Ecclesiology in a Post-Modern Context* (New York: Oxford University Press, 1999), 13.

85. Douglas John Hall, "Metamorphosis: From Christendom to Diaspora," in *Confident Witness–Changing World: Rediscovering the Gospel in North America,* ed. Craig Van Gelder (Grand Rapids: Eerdmans, 1999), 77.

86. Ibid., 71.

87. Michael S. Horton, *People and Place: A Covenant Ecclesiology* (Louisville: Westminster John Knox, 2008), 177.

2

The Church as Word-Event

These next three chapters present and critically engage various theological accounts of the church. To reclaim a theologically grounded identity for the church, we must begin with God. The church is not primarily something we do, but something that God is doing and creating in and through us. Therefore, each of these models will have a theological starting point: God's word of promise addressed to us, the communion of the Triune God's being, and the mission of the Triune God (*missio Dei*).

This first paradigm is rooted in the Reformation insight that the church is a "creature of the word." This understanding of the church begins with the word: God's address to humanity in the living Christ (the Word) and the proclamation of the gospel of Jesus Christ. The proclamation of the gospel and the administration of the sacraments in accord with this gospel constitute an "event" that presupposes a reception by the community in whose midst they are occurring. This simultaneously creates the "event" of the church, whose being is being recreated and actualized continuously through proclamation of the gospel. Avery Dulles, in his classic work *Models of the Church*,[1] sees it as the classic Protestant model of the church. Its chief proponents were the neo-orthodox theologians in the mid-twentieth century, in particular Karl Barth, and many theologians continue to present it as the traditional Reformation view of the church.

There is not one "word ecclesiology," but several. What they have in common is their theological starting point—God's address to us in the Word and our encounter with that Word, the living Christ who is made present to the believer in the *kerygma*, the proclamation of the gospel—and a preference for speaking of the church in terms of activity rather than being and structure. The church is described in terms of the activities of hearing and gathering; the church is the assembly of those who have heard the promise through word and sacrament. For the proponents of this concept, the church is a verb, not a noun. For some, this model is almost as constitutive of Protestantism as the doctrine of justification. A dynamic concept of the church is seen as necessary to protect the freedom of the gospel from the dangers of institutionalization and authoritarianism.

HISTORICAL BACKGROUND

The idea of the church as a "creature of the Word"[2] originated with Martin Luther. As noted in chapter 1, the twin questions guiding the Reformation were "Where do I find a gracious God?" and "Where is the true church?" These questions coalesced for Luther in a third question: Who or what has the final authority to assure me that I am in God's grace?[3] As Markus Wriedt points out, in order to understand Luther's own ecclesiological development, it is important to understand that his starting point was that of late medieval ecclesiology, in particular the question of final or ultimate authority. In the two centuries leading up to Luther's reform, the doctrine of the church had become a central concern among late medieval theologians with the appearance of several tracts entitled *De Ecclesia*. These tracts were concerned with determining the "true church" and the locus and foundation of the church's authority. This quest and the intensity with which it was undertaken were "sparked by a crisis of confidence in the papal hierarchy which began in the thirteenth century with the challenge of the Waldensians and the Franciscan Spirituals."[4] In each of these tracts, however, the ultimate locus of authority remained some concept of the "true church," though one defined apart from the institutional structure, for example, as the true remnant or the elect.[5]

Where Luther departed from the medieval tradition and these early reformers was in pointing *not* to the church—however alternatively defined or reformed—but solely to the word of God, that is, the promise of salvation, the living gospel. For Luther, the answer to the quest of the "true church" was this: the true church could and did exist wherever the word was being truly proclaimed and nourishing the faithful. Underlying Luther's thinking was a deep pastoral concern.[6] Luther worried that the church was not feeding the Christian faithful with the promise of the gospel in the midst of the various crises, economic, social, and spiritual, that faced late medieval Christendom.[7] Luther believed that the church must be put back under the authority of the word so that believers in Christendom could hear the gospel proclaimed and be comforted by the good news.

This led Luther to challenge the institutional definition of the church that had developed at that point in history. In medieval Roman Catholicism, the church was the perfect society marked by a particular structure and sacramental system that was dependent on that structure—that is, holy orders, episcopacy, papacy. But according to Luther, this structure had not guaranteed the right proclamation of the gospel (that is, justification by grace through faith), which led to the aforementioned pastoral and ecclesiological crisis. For the Reformers, the authority of the church could no longer be guaranteed by its external structures and offices which, according to the Catholic apologists, embodied the classical marks of the church (for instance, unity and apostolicity coming together in the offices of bishop and pope), but only by the right proclamation of the word and right administration of the sacraments, means through which the promise of salvation was given to the faithful. For the Reformers, then, the true church could only be marked or identified externally by word and sacrament. The question "Where is the church?" was answered in medieval Christendom with "Where the pope is, where the bishops and priests are," and so forth. The Reformers offered a new answer: "Where the word of God is being preached and promised in the sacraments."

Not only is the word of God the *one indispensible true mark* of the church, it is "the food which sustains the believers" and "the foundation upon which the Church has been founded."[8] Luther developed this idea most systematically in "Concerning the Ministry" (1523), which culminates in his statement that "since the Church owes its birth to the Word, is nourished, aided and strengthened by it, it is obvious that it cannot be without the Word. If it is without the Word it ceases to be a Church."[9] According to Paul Althaus, for Luther, "only the proclamation of the word is necessary to create the church . . . the church is nothing else than the miracle of the power of the word constantly appearing in a new form."[10] The International Lutheran-Catholic Dialogue (1994), *Church and Justification*, concurs: "Consequently, the main ecclesiological concern of the Reformation was perpetual dependence on the gospel and subordination to it. This was concentrated in the formula that the church is *creatura Evangelii*."[11]

Thus, for Luther, the church is created by the word of God; it is a "creature of the Word" because it owes its very existence to the life-giving word of the gospel. But what does this creaturely existence look like for the church and its members? From his earliest lectures on the Psalms, Luther discovered and held on to the insight that "the church is a 'people,' 'God's people,' the 'community of believers,' the '*communio sanctorum*.'"[12] Scott Hendrix notes that the major shift Luther made from his medieval predecessors was not to speak of the church in terms of the people of God, "the faithful."[13] Nor was it to emphasize a "spiritual" church over a "visible church."[14] The medieval tradition taught that the truly faithful are invisible because one cannot discern whether a particular believer is in a state of grace, that is, possesses the definitive *caritas* ("selfless love") that requires and depends on the sacramental system. What was new is the way that Luther defined the invisible character of the truly faithful. Luther's study of the Psalms led him to understand that Christ is present in "the faithful" not through *caritas*, but through faith. This makes the character of the church "hidden." As Hendrix notes, however, "The hidden character of the church does not apply so much to the persons of the 'faithful' themselves as to their orientation in faith and the spirit, which are intangible entities, and yet whose possession leads to a way of life that is actually quite visible. This orientation, this life in faith and the spirit directed toward invisible, spiritual goods, is the mark of the true [faithful]."[15]

Hendrix argues that Luther made this shift from *caritas* to faith on the basis of a hermeneutical understanding of letter/spirit. Specifically, Luther defines "spiritual" in terms of orientation: the carnal person (or people) is oriented toward and puts trust in worldly things, the spiritual person (or people) in spiritual, invisible things.[16] This hermeneutical understanding had ecclesiological implications. If believers must possess *caritas* to remain truly faithful, their life depends on the sacramental grace administered by priests. Faith as orientation toward invisible goods does not rely on a particular, external structure of the church.[17] Believers can exist in any external community, as long as faith is nurtured there through the word or promise of God. At the same time, faith must be nurtured in a community; while faith is individually appropriated it is never individualistic.[18] Wilhelm Pauck agrees that Luther's view is personalist without being individualistic, because of Luther's emphasis on the church as a fellowship of mutual self-giving love. Indeed, for Luther "to be a Christian and to be in the church, the community of believers, is one and the same."[19]

Thus what is created by the word is an assembly—an assembly of hearts united in faith—but this is not the same thing as saying that the assembly is invisible, or that the "creaturely" aspects of the church's existence are epiphenomenal or irrelevant to the church's self-understanding. For Luther, it primarily means that the church receives its orientation, life, nourishment not from orders and structure, but from what is spiritual and cannot be seen, that is, the word of God given through the Spirit.[20] It is also important to keep in mind what Luther was protesting, namely, as Bernhard Lohse notes, "the way in which the papacy had, for all practical purposes, set aside the gospel in the church. Luther was not protesting against the external nature of the church itself, nor did he understand Christendom as 'invisible.'"[21] What is invisible is God's action in creating the church. Only as a *creatura verbi* is the church an object of faith. "But," as Christoph Schwöbel points out, "the human actions made possible by God's invisible constitution of the church are very much visible—and according to Luther—even more audible."[22]

In summary, the concept of the church as "creature of the Word" developed in response to the context of late medieval Christianity, where the church's being and authority were guaranteed by a particular institutional structure and hierarchy of holy orders. The church receives its orientation from the word, not any office in the church; it is the authority of God's word, not the church, through which we are assured of God's gracious favor toward us. This same word of promise also creates the church: the community that is brought into birth through the word which, at the same time, becomes the "mother" through which others hear the same gospel promise in word and sacrament.[23]

The Church as Word-Event

Veli-Matti Kärkkäinen sees the idea of the church as "word-event" as a natural development of the trajectory started by Luther. The Lutheran Reformation "had from the start an actualist understanding of the church: 'the church is something *going on* in the world.'"[24] I argue, however, that this is more of a development than simple reclamation of the Reformers' ecclesiology. Luther articulated his ideas in response to concerns regarding the "true church." As this concept developed in the twentieth century, one sees a shift from the focus on the word as the guarantee of the presence of the "true church" to an idea of the church itself as a "word-event," or the word in action. This new concept retains the focus on God's creative action in creating the church by the word, but is in danger of neglecting the communal aspects of the church's existence.

Avery Dulles refers to this model as "Church as Herald" in his influential book *Models of the Church*, naming Karl Barth as its chief proponent. This concept and Barth's appropriation of it would come to influence many American Protestant theologians in the twentieth century. Dulles summarizes the Herald model this way: "The word of God is not a substance immanent in the Church, but rather an event that takes place as often as God addresses his people and is believed. The Church therefore is actually constituted by the word being proclaimed and faithfully heard. The Church is the congregation that is gathered by the word—a word that ceaselessly summons it to repentance and reform."[25]

THE CONTEXT FOR BARTH'S ECCLESIOLOGY

Dulles does not address the contextual factors that contributed to the retrieval of this church concept by neoorthodox theologians in the twentieth century. There was still a concern over how one might discern the "true church," but the context in which this question was being asked was quite different from Luther's day. While Barth did not begin his theological method with an explicit reflection on his context, his ecclesiology was still contextual. Barth addressed the situation that the churches found themselves in during the rise of the Nationalist Social State in Germany.[26]

The German Church Struggle was as much against the German Christian Party as it was against the Nationalist Socialist State.[27] Edmund Schlink speaks of the struggle in terms of reclaiming the confession of the true gospel in the face of false teachings. In combining Christian teachings with the tenets of National Socialism, the German Christians had "camouflaged" their persecution of the church and the Jews, by claiming to represent "positive Christianity" against "godless Bolshevism."[28] The totalitarian state suppressed the church and distorted the true teaching of the gospel into false doctrine with the anti-Christian myth of the neopagan Nazi cult and its doctrinal distortions.[29]

The German Church Struggle brought to light the truth about the faith of the German Christians. Their apostasy was evident, both in terms of their easy conscience in the face of persecution of others and of the loss of the sense of the gospel's urgency. Also, "the church had become more bourgeois than had been realized. God had been thought of as the protector of an ordered family life," the guarantor of a nation and race.[30] The church was revealed to be little more than an empty shell, its teachings co-opted by the National Socialist State and devoid of the living gospel. The German Church Struggle was the catalyst that awakened the faith of the people and inspired a theological understanding of the church based on the "power of the word" alone and not natural theology or "orders of creation." In a memorandum entitled "Church Opposition 1933" delivered to the Pastors' Emergency League on November 15, 1933, Barth wrote that the protest against the heresy of the German Christians must be "fundamentally directed against the source of all single errors, namely that the 'German Christians' assert Germany nationality, its history and its political present, as a second source of revelation *beside* Holy Scripture as the only source of revelation, and thereby show themselves to be believers in 'another God.'"[31] What was needed was a dynamic ecclesiology grounded not in natural theology or orders of creation, but solely in the event of God's word as address to humanity.

THE CHURCH AS WORD-EVENT IN BARTH'S ECCLESIOLOGY

Although one can discern a development in Barth's doctrine of the church, one can see three interrelated ideas woven throughout: the word as God's address to humanity, God's act of election through the word, and the church as the "event" created by the word.[32] As Kent Knutson states, the idea of the church as "event" is related to Barth's dynamic concept of revelation, itself an "event through which God speaks to [human beings]; and the primary mode for this event is the preaching of the Word."[33] Although the basis for the Christian faith is the word of God, it only becomes real proclamation when it is preached. Barth's concept of the church naturally follows from this prolegomena. "The Church *is* when it takes place, and it takes place in the form of a sequence and nexus of definite human activities,"[34] most centrally the event of proclamation. Specifically, the church itself is an "event" that consists in the gathering of the elect who are called to be witnesses and heralds to Christ's victory over death and the grave.[35] The German word used by Barth is *ereignis*, and by it Barth means "that the church is not constituted once for all, but is continually being recreated by renewed divine activity."[36]

Some interpreters of Barth worry that this is an actualistic understanding that could lead to a view of the church as a "discontinuous 'gathered' community" or "succession of events without any real continuity"[37] beyond the constancy of the identity of the One who gathers the church. For Barth, however, the event that constitutes the church takes place in a specific location, a congregation.[38] For Barth, a congregation refers not merely to a building or a community, but to a living congregation, "which consists in the event by which it is gathered together: that is, the congregation is the decisive element in this final phase in the story of God's relations with man."[39] In his mature ecclesiology, Barth explicitly brings together the idea of church as "event" with church as fellowship, as the gathered are "fused together in the common action of the Word which they have heard into a definite human fellowship,"[40] the church as congregation, and church as a community that endures through time.[41]

As Kimlyn Bender notes, Barth's willingness to speak of the church in historical terms did not lead him to abandon his prior understanding of the church as an event that must be constituted again and again through the work of the Holy Spirit.[42] The church is both an event and a history; these aspects exist in a dialectical relation: "The historical and enduring existence of the church exists only insofar, paradoxically, as it is an ever-new event."[43]

The historical community that is constituted by event is also constituted by the decree that made them the elect people of God together in the first place. Here Barth's Reformed sensibilities come to the fore, but with a twist. The church is grounded in God's act, which is to elect through the Word, the living Christ. The church itself is viewed as part of God's eternal covenantal intention; it must be understood primarily in theological terms, as a result of the action of God, rather than humans.[44] Barth describes the election of the church as a whole, not only as the sum of the election of individuals. As Bender points out, "The church for Barth is established by an eternal decree, and its own election stands under the election of Jesus Christ while preceding the election of the individual believer. The church thus stands between Christ and the Christian."[45] In other words, for Barth, election first refers to the election of Jesus Christ, then to the community, and then only finally to the individual believer.

THE EXISTENTIALIST TURN TO FAITH

Dulles also treats the mid-twentieth-century existential variants of this model, including Rudolf Bultmann and Gerhard Ebeling. These theologians understood the "word-event" primarily in existential terms, between God and the believer. They emphasized the present impact of God's address on the individual believer and her standing before God. Whereas Barth was concerned with the truth of the word of God for theology and ecclesiology, Bultmann was concerned to make *sola fide*, or more specifically, the "decision for faith," the "last irreducible point of the theological structure."[46]

Thus the focus came to be more on the event of preaching through which the person encounters the word and less on the community and fellowship that is created by the word-event. The point of departure for Bultmann's existential project "was his assured situation as 'hearer' of the Word. The development of the project was to consist in an 'actualization' of the gospel for the 'man of today.'"[47] This reframes the distinct Protestant idea of the church as the creature of the word in terms of an understanding of language whereby language does something, creates something. One does not determine the nature of words by asking what they mean, but by asking what they effect or set in motion.[48] What the word effects in the first place, of course, is faith. The word of God is present "where the communication of God's Word takes place, here and now, in the concrete communication of faith."[49] For Ebeling, the church is best described not as the sphere of faith, but as the "summons to faith. It *is* this event of faith" because the central event that defines the church is the proclamation of the word of God which summons people to faith.[50]

The existentialist shift makes the "event" of the word more narrowly focused than we saw in Barth's theology. The church is described less as the "sphere of faith" (that is, as a community through which the Spirit works to create faith) and more as the "event of faith itself," which leads to a more individualistic focus and suggests a more instrumentalist view of the church. The danger in this variant of the word-event ecclesiology is that faith—and not the word—becomes constitutive of the church. While this may not be the intention of the existentialists, by focusing on the individual's encounter of faith they are in danger of neglecting the communal reality of the church.

GERHARD FORDE'S "PROCLAMATION ECCLESIOLOGY"

The word-event paradigm continues to be influential in Lutheran and Reformed theological circles in North America. In Lutheranism, one can see the influence of the Barthian word-event concept in the theology of the late Gerhard O. Forde and many of his former students. Forde's ideas had a significant impact on American Lutheranism and the debates in the Evangelical Lutheran Church in America over ecclesiology, ministry, and ecumenical agreements.[51] Forde believed the church had lost its bearing by failing to proclaim the radical nature of the gospel, a failure he attributed to modern society's lack of reverence for the law.[52] The attack on the law means that liberalism is dying or, more likely, is already dead, because "liberalism is nothing without its faith, without the belief that the *telos* toward which man strives is the true 'ethical commonwealth' where there is a perfect wedding between natural inclination and law, where man spontaneously and freely does the good for the sake of the good."[53]

Forde agrees with G. W. F. Hegel that in order to get beyond Kantian moralism, a negation of the law is required; however, this negation cannot be accomplished by human beings, whether Hegel's Absolute Spirit immanent in human society and human spirit, or Marx's revolution. Only God can negate the law; this is an eschatological event that happened on the cross. This divine negation stands against the official optimism of modern culture. Thus it is not surprising that the church has found itself co-opted by both the antinomian response to "problem of the law," on the one hand (as can be seen in much of contemporary ecclesial ethics), and by crusades for moralism or justice (as can be seen in the alignment of churches with right-wing political agendas or liberal social movements), on the other.[54]

Like Barth, Forde describes the word of God as an event in which God acts; however, unlike for the existentialists, the word-event does not cause a crisis of decision. For Forde, the word of God slays and brings sinners to life.[55] Law and gospel are the means by which this divine negation happens. The law confronts the sinner with the fact that she is lost and can do nothing about her situation. The gospel is a "whole new way of hearing, an entirely new dimension of life; it is a word which is full of promise, which makes all of life blossom with the good news."[56] Because Luther understood Paul's spirit/letter distinction in 1 Corinthians 3:6 to refer to two kinds of preaching and hearing (rather than two meanings in the text, one spiritual and one literal), Luther can offer a new hermeneutical approach "toward an understanding of the Word as active, as doing something to us."[57] In other words, the spirit is not some inner level of meaning that is reached by the interpreter, but is the Spirit of God itself, who as Forde states "comes precisely in and through the letter, the text, the proclamation of it, to kill and to make alive."[58]

This makes proclamation or preaching the proper *Sitz im Leben* for the law/gospel hermeneutic.[59] By proclamation, Forde means the "explicit declaration of the good news, the gospel, the kerygma" as a word from God. The old law speaks of Christ in the imperative; the gospel speaks in a declarative mood, whereby the proclamation delivers to the hearer "a first-to-second person unconditional promise authorized by what occurs in Jesus Christ according to the scriptures."[60] Indeed, God is only revealed in the "concrete proclamation, the present-tense Word from God, spoken 'to you' the listener."[61]

Proclamation is closely tied to election in Forde's thought. The biblical narrative tells the story of God's election, a story that began when God chose Israel and then came "in Jesus to break down the wall of separation between Jew and Gentile so that election shall know no bounds."[62] This story continues through the ministry of the church and its proclamation. God elects through proclamation, enjoining "those who hear, believe, and follow to speak of the Word of God, to go and do the electing."[63] Forde criticizes those like Barth who attempted to "solve" the problem of election through universalizing tendencies. Rather than try to explain or dismiss the electing God, the proper recourse is proclamation. Forde states, "Since God is an electing God, the only real solution to the problem of being un-reconciled to the God not preached is to do the deed of the preached God: 'Once you were lost but now you are found.'"[64]

While Barth describes the event of the cross in terms of a revelation of God's love and mercy for the sinner, for Forde it is the act by which God's wrath is put to an end.[65] This happens on the cross in what Forde calls the great reversal. The cross, Forde says, "spells not only the death of Jesus but the death of the sinner. Jesus' death is not a substitution for our death; it is our death."[66] The cross is necessary because in order for new life to begin, the old self must die. The new order or reality introduced by the event of the cross is the eschatological kingdom and the gospel is the announcement of this wholly other resurrection future.[67] Forde states emphatically that "the divine pronouncement of justification for Jesus' sake *is* the death and the new life. To believe the message of justification is to die and be raised to newness of life."[68]

The church is called into being by this very same proclamation. Forde describes the church primarily as an assembly of hearers, who having heard and received the good news of their election, "undertake to speak again what they have heard, give what has been received, and make appropriate arrangements to do so."[69] In this way, Forde speaks of the church as an event that "*occurs* where the quite specific activity known as speaking the gospel occurs and the sacraments are administered according to that gospel. Where that does not occur there is no such thing as the church of Jesus Christ."[70] Forde emphasizes the *peccator* (sinful) aspect of Luther's *simul*: the church is a company of sinners who lives "from the concrete, present-tense proclamation. It will know that it cannot live today on yesterday's gospel. It must hear again and again and assembles so to hear and takes what steps it can to guarantee that it will indeed hear the gospel."[71] The church always lives in hope of a promise yet to be fulfilled. Forde's hesitancy to emphasize the *iustus* (justified) aspect is related to his understanding of sanctification as "getting used to justification." The church does not experience holiness except in relation to a promise that it anticipates eschatologically.

For Forde, the *satis est* ("it is enough") clause of Article VII of the central Lutheran symbol, the Augsburg Confession (1530), points to an "eschatological understanding of the church" by taking account of the eschatological distinction between the ages. The point of this clause is to set an eschatological limit to what can be claimed by the institutional forms of the church in this age. This results in a suspicion of all ecclesial forms beyond the local congregation and the claim that the church "should be understood strictly as a this-age entity. What comes after the church in this world, that for which the faithful hope, is the Kingdom of God."[72]

To safeguard the eschatological character of the gospel, Forde follows the Reformers in speaking of the church as both hidden and revealed, which he prefers to the more common dialectic of visible and invisible, because the language of invisibility suggests a Platonic ideal against which the Reformers strenuously argued. The church is hidden both in fact and necessity: because the hearing of faith is not directly discernible in this age, and to prevent the tyranny of institutional church.[73] However, the church is at the same time revealed or made visible by its two marks, the preaching of word and the administration of the sacraments as well as the bearing of the cross. Forde writes, "The true church lives under the sign of the cross and can assert its authority in no way other than that of its Lord: revelation under a form of opposites, humility, service, suffering death."[74]

Thus, for Forde, the true or hidden church exists only eschatologically as an article of faith. On this side of the eschaton, it can only be defined by the events that announce the eschatological promise: the proclamation of the word and the administration of the sacraments in the gathered community. Like Barth before him, Forde defines the church as an event that occurs when these things happen. He understands the *satis est* clause not only to be a statement about what is necessary for the unity of the church, but also what is enough for the church's "being." The church exists dynamically in the proclamation of the promise of the forgiveness of sins. Not only does Forde reject definitions of the church that are based on external structures and order (here following Luther), but also those based on any characteristic beyond the sheer proclamation of the word (here going beyond Luther). Forde fears that to point to anything other than what God is doing through the event of proclamation in the assembly will lead to triumphalism.

Although for Forde the church is "the body of believers that has been called into being *by the gospel*,"[75] he avoids using not only institutional but also organic and communal language to describe the body, preferring more functional or collective phrases like "the company of those who have been put to death and raised in Christ," or church as "outpost" of the new age whose way can "never be readily comprehensible to this age" and whose "existence is a matter of faith."[76] This seems contrary to the New Testament witness that describes the "way" of new life shared by the Christians in terms of *koinonia, liturgia,* and *diakonia,* in addition to *kerygma.* Forde's hesitancy to describe this "way" of new life is rooted, of course, in his concern to safeguard the alien nature of Christ's righteousness and the eschatological reality of the new life promised in Christ. Indeed, Forde's ecclesiology seems to leave no room for the work of the Holy Spirit until the eschaton, except in securing faith for the individual believer. Neither is there any sense of church being sent out by the Spirit. In fact, Forde is wary of any talk of "mission" applied to the church. He argues that it is too often the case that mission and evangelism emphases in the church water down the theological content of the gospel, on the one hand, and too easily buy into human notions of progress, on the other.[77]

MICHAEL HORTON'S COVENANT ECCLESIOLOGY

Michael Horton, an emerging voice in Reformed circles, offers another recent example of a word-event or "speech-act" ecclesiology. While Horton's Reformed sensibilities are apparent throughout his work, his approach to ecclesiology is strikingly similar to Forde's. Horton believes that one of the legacies of the Enlightenment is the twofold idea that the self is radically autonomous and the solution to our problems lies within ourselves. Modern theology has woefully lacked the resources to address this situation because of its own anthropocentrism. The only theology that has anything to offer to the world is a theology that begins with God and God's address to human beings. Specifically, we need a word outside of ourselves because we need a salvation outside of ourselves.[78] Horton writes, "In the face of various attempts (whether ancient, modern, or postmodern) to domesticate God's transcendent word through an autonomous mastery, the church desperately needs to recover its confidence in the sacramental word that comes to us from outside of us to make all things new."[79] Horton is especially critical of church-growth consultants, like George Barna, who seem to place all of the emphasis on what individuals do; there is no suggestion in this literature that the church might be defined by God's work for us.[80]

Thus Horton sees theology not as a comprehensive science of being and things, but "as the speech about God as he has revealed himself in Word and act, especially in the person of Jesus Christ."[81] The word is living, active, and dynamic and always encounters us from outside of ourselves.[82] This is covenantal speech that summons the self to relationship with God. Within the context of the covenant, God speaks (and the believer hears) a word of both command (law) and promise (gospel). With Forde, he sees the law and gospel as the means by which the Holy Spirit effects what is promised;[83] thus the theologian's primary concern is not to ask what the text means, but to ask what the speech is trying to do.[84]

It is this emphasis on the external word as the medium of God's saving action that distinguished the Reformers not only from the Roman Catholics, but also the Enthusiasts.[85] The word is the means through which God communicates, in the present, the saving benefits of the past event of Christ's life, death, and resurrection to the hearer.[86] Thus Horton affirms with Luther that the church is the creation of the word, a notion which "arises from the repeated assumption in scripture that God's speaking is acting, and this acting is not only descriptive and propositional; it is also creative and performative."[87] This activity, Horton stresses, is solely God's; therefore the idea of the church as the creature of the word "disputes every claim that prioritizes human agency (individual or corporate) over divine agency."[88]

Horton appeals to the linguistic turn of late modernity and speech-act theory to develop further his understanding of divine action and speech.[89] The community can only receive its identity through the covenant offered by God, the story that narrates a community's identity through a series of events that the community did not create and over which it has no control. Indeed, the elect are "created by speech, upheld by speech, redeemed by speech, and one day glorified by speech; we are, like the rest of creation, summoned beings, not autonomous. We exist because we have been spoken into existence, and we persist in time because the Spirit ensures that the Father's speaking, in the Son, will not return void."[90]

By placing the law/gospel hermeneutic within the broader paradigm of covenant, Horton allows for a more positive role of the law in the Christian life whereby the law not only accuses of sin but also provides guidance for the human response to the covenant of grace.[91] In terms of the "word-event" paradigm, this means that the "illocutionary power" of God's speaking evokes a response both of trust in God's promise and obedience to God's commands. However, Horton stresses that God gives the elect what is needed in order to receive their identity as God's people and to respond in trust and obedience.

It is in and through every event of word and sacrament that God establishes the covenant, and which in turn constitutes the hearers into "a people, a new nation of servants who listen and hear, rather than belonging to the old nation of lords, who, 'having ears cannot listen.'"[92] With Forde, Horton agrees that the only visible "marks" of the church are the word proclaimed and the sacraments administered, which in turn can tell us "where" the church is and where grace can be found. Horton, however, is more willing than Forde to address the "who" of the church. The word and the sacraments mark both the place where the church is, that is, the place where the covenant speaking is happening and creating, and also the people created by this event, that is, a covenant community. Although Roman Catholicism has characteristically emphasized church as place (marked by a particular structure) and evangelicals and Pentecostals generally think of church in terms of people (marked by a certain way of life), in both cases, Horton asserts, "the emphasis is placed on the church as actor more than receiver."[93] A covenantal approach, however, can affirm the church both as "place" and "people" because of the emphasis on God's action in word and sacrament.

Horton distinguishes his covenantal approach from what he sees as two extremes in contemporary ecclesiology: one that distinguishes the invisible from the visible church as historical institution to the point of seeing them as two different entities; and the other which collapses the head and members into a single subject, the *totus Christus*.[94] Instead, Horton proposes covenant as the mediating category for how Christ is present in the gathered community. The church emerges in the place where the risen one has ascended and sends the Spirit, enabling the risen Christ to be "present in the world *through* the community, though not *as* the community."[95] Because of the eschatological distinction between the two ages, this "place" is not identical with the risen body of Christ, but is that through which Christ is present to the world.[96] A covenantal account of the relationship between the head and members of the church as the one body of Christ allows for distinction without separation and is sensitive to the eschatological tension between the already and the not yet.

Horton further explores the identity and mission of the covenant community using the other three creedal attributes (holy, catholic, apostolic). In each case, he treats them in a way that highlights God as actor and the church as recipient. For example, in a covenant approach, holiness emerges not from the corporate body or its members, but "from the ministry of the Son and the Spirit, sent from the Father, working through Word and Sacraments."[97] The church is holy insofar as it witnesses to Christ; holiness is never the possession of the members. Horton explores catholicity in light of the Reformed doctrine of election. Ecclesial being is lodged "in God's electing grace, rather than to the extent to which local churches actually correspond to the consummated kingdom."[98] On this basis, he offers a challenge to the widespread tendency of many churches to appeal to the homogeneity (especially in terms of socioeconomic location) principle in order to grow. Such "rival catholicities" should never be allowed to determine ecclesial character. The location that is decisive for Christians is "in Christ."[99]

Horton also addresses apostolicity in light of covenant. He criticizes the actualistic tendencies in Barth's ecclesiology, arguing that because "a covenant community takes time, it cannot be merely an event, much less a crater that is left behind by revelation. Both a people (*synaxis*) and a place (*ekklēsia*), an event and an institution, the visible communion today is connected historically to the apostles by the external marks of the Word, sacrament, and discipline."[100] Renewing the covenant through the means given to the church, word and sacrament (and discipline), is the active work of the Holy Spirit. Horton discusses this attribute primarily in terms of the apostolic ministry rather than the apostolic mission, or the sending of the church. He defines mission primarily in terms of the ministry of word and sacrament to the gathered[101] and is critical of much current missional literature for not recognizing that God is the one in charge of the church's mission.[102]

An Assessment of Contemporary Word Ecclesiologies

This word-event paradigm offers a clear theological starting point for a doctrine of the church and, as such, addresses one major concern of this work: that ecclesiology should begin with who God is and what God is doing. A particular strength of this model for many mainline Protestants is, of course, its strong Reformation heritage. Contemporary word-event ecclesiologies draw on the Reformation insight that the church is a creature of the word, not only in that the church originates from God's word, but also that the church is continually sustained by God's word, a word that addresses it from outside of itself in order to bring life, salvation, and forgiveness of sins. This model is also clear about the primary task of the church: to bear God's word in and to the world. The church was not created to be a social club, but for the sake of the word's continued proclamation. It may be tempting to describe this view of the church as functional, but this is not quite correct. To be sure, Forde prefers "act" language (and Horton "speech-act") over "being" language; however, it is important to remember that for both, the primary actor is God. The church is not defined by what it does so much as what it receives. Both define the church first and foremost by its reception of God's promises. The church is described in passive terms, first as a people to whom gospel speaking happens and, secondarily, as a people called to proclaim the same eschatological gospel of promise.[103] The church exists between this age and the next and lives in anticipation of eschatological fullness; therefore we must be careful what we can claim about this community in the present.

The Barthian shift from viewing the church as a creature of the word to a "word-event" puts the focus more on the event of the word than on the community created by that event. This can lead to an overly narrow focus on the individual hearing of the word, in terms of an individual existential encounter that runs the risk of losing the communal aspects of ecclesial identity. In fact, Forde's theology does not really need a doctrine of the church as much as a preaching office.[104] By so strongly emphasizing the "word" that creates (and the faith that the word engenders in believers' hearts), Forde has little to say about the community that is created by the word. Even if the word-event paradigm could be expanded to include an understanding of the church as event *outside* of the traditional setting of pulpit and altar, the emphasis on "what is happening" over and against "who is there" can lead to a functional concept of the church that does not address the very real quest for authentic community in today's context. This is driven by the desire to protect the alien nature of Christ's righteousness and the sovereignty of the word that always addresses us from outside of ourselves. However, not addressing the creaturely aspect of the community which is created by the word can lead to the idea that the community itself is epiphenomenal, which has no biblical support. This model's strong focus on the word gives clear theological content, but no fleshed-out ecclesiology, and ironically opens itself to a sociological definition of the church, even though that is not its intention.[105] Ecclesiology should address not only the origin of the church and how it is marked by word and sacrament, but the kind of "creature" the church is and is called to be in order to participate in God's purposes. Horton has more to say about the creaturely aspect of the church, including the human response to God's covenant-making speech and action. God's covenant of grace is absolute and unconditional, but it does give rise to a genuine covenantal partnership. But here, too, the emphasis is mostly on the community that is gathered and individual obedience to God's word in covenant partnership.

By rooting the church as event in the event of word and sacrament—and in particular the hearing of the word—both Forde and Horton strongly emphasize the church as the gathered community. In one sense, both are answering the Reformation question, "Where is the church?" with the classic Reformation answer of "where the word is rightly preached and the sacraments rightly administered." The true church is not the activist church, the church where people draw attention to their good works, and so forth, but the church where the word (specifically the gospel promise) is regularly being proclaimed and the sacraments rightly administered. The church is described as an event of God's speaking; the driving question is, "Where do we hear the gospel? Where do we encounter God's word that slays/makes alive—that draws us into the covenant?" One might ask whether their question is primarily about the church proper or about the human condition. In both cases, the church becomes instrumental to the drama of salvation (Horton) or the "killing and making alive" of the sinner (Forde). Although Horton is also interested in exploring the church's identity and mission, as we have seen, for Horton mission is described in terms of the gathered, not sent-out, church.

Both focus more on what this means for those already gathered and less on what it means for the world. The question reflects not only Reformation roots, but the Christendom context of the Reformation. To ask the question "Where can I find the church?" assumes that people know that God does have a word for us, that there is a promise or covenant God wishes to give. It assumes that people are seeking to find the true church in which to hear the gospel; it presumes that people are looking for a church in which to hear the gospel. It supposes that people know that the church is the people to whom and the place where this gospel promise will be offered. But how does this promise move out from the gathered community to those who do not yet know? How will they know that the Spirit desires to gather them into the church and preach the gospel to them?

For all of his insights regarding the current challenges facing the church, Horton does not engage the challenges and questions posed by an increasingly post-Christendom context in which more and more people are not raised as Christians and have no opportunity hear the gospel. Rather than "Where is the true church—or even, simply, the church?," the question facing the church is a post-Christendom context is, "Why the church?" The question is no longer "What church should I attend?" but "Why even bother?" To engage the question "why," the church needs to know first of all who it is, which is a community that is not only gathered but also sent into the world. A Spirit-breathed ecclesiology offers a concept of the church in which the Spirit both gathers the church by the word and also sends the church into the world in a kind of elliptical movement in God's drama of salvation. If the people of God are not sent into the world, how will others hear the good news? By operating with certain assumptions of Christendom, contemporary word ecclesiologies tend to focus on the Spirit's work in *gathering* the church, and not on the Spirit's work in *sending* the church.

FOR REFLECTION AND DISCUSSION

1. What new "question" does Martin Luther ask—and how does it shape his ecclesiology? Why is it incorrect to say that Luther believed in an "invisible church?"
2. What are the central elements of the word-event paradigm?
3. How do Karl Barth and the existentialists develop Luther's idea of the church as a "creature of the Word?"
4. How do Gerhard Forde and Michael Horton further develop the concept of the church as a "word-event" in their ecclesiologies? What similarities and differences do you see in these authors, especially with regard to the identity and purpose/mission of the church?
5. What are the contributions of the word-event paradigm to the ecclesiological discussion today, especially for those with Reformation roots? How does starting with the "word" help you

think differently about the identity and purpose of the church in today's context? What elements of this paradigm should be retained for a contemporary ecclesiology for post-Christendom age? How would your congregation respond to the ideas in this paradigm?

6. What are the weaknesses of this paradigm? Does it sufficiently address the challenges of the post-Christendom context in which the church finds itself? Why or why not?

Notes

1. Avery Dulles, *Models of the Church*, exp. ed. (New York: Doubleday, 2002).

2. Luther explicitly called the church a creature of the Word in "The Babylonian Captivity of the Church," in *Luther's Works,* vol. 36, trans. Frederick C. Ahrens, ed. Helmut T. Lehmann and Abdel Ross Wentz (Philadelphia: Fortress Press, 1959), 107.

3. Marcus Wriedt, "Luther on Call and Ordination," *Concordia Journal* 28, no. 3 (2002): 258.

4. Scott Hendrix, "In Quest of the *Vera Ecclesia*: The Crises of Late Medieval Ecclesiology," *Viator* 7 (1976): 349.

5. William of Ockham, for example, tried to locate the true church in a remnant of faithful Christians who could continue to exist apart from the Roman hierarchy. See ibid., 360–64.

6. Bernhard Lohse, *Martin Luther: An Introduction to his Life and Work,* trans. Robert C. Schultz (Minneapolis: Fortress Press, 1986), 41.

7. Hendrix, "In Quest of the *Vera Ecclesia*," 351, 376.

8. George W. Forell, *The Reality of the Church as the Communion of Saints: A Study of Luther's Doctrine of the Church* (Wenonah, NJ: by the author, 1943), 78.

9. Martin Luther, "Concerning the Ministry, 1523," in *Luther's Works*, vol. 40, trans. and ed. Conrad Bergendoff (Philadelphia: Fortress Press, 1958), 37.

10. Paul Althaus, *The Theology of Martin Luther*, trans. Robert C. Schultz (Philadelphia: Fortress Press, 1966), 290.

11. *Church and Justification: Understanding the Church in Light of Justification*, Lutheran-Catholic International Joint Commission (Geneva: Lutheran World Federation, 1994), 2.4.1 §36.

12. Wilhelm Pauck, *The Heritage of the Reformation*, rev. ed. (Glencoe, IL: Free Press, 1961), 31.

13. Since the time of Thomas Aquinas, theologians described the church as the body of the faithful. For most medieval theologians this description functioned as an alternative description of the hierarchical, institutional church. See John Tonkin, *The Church and the Secular Order in Reformation Thought* (New York: Columbia University Press, 1971), 18.

14. Scott Hendrix, *Ecclesia in Via: Ecclesiological Developments in the Medieval Psalm Exegesis and the "Dictata Super Psalterium" (1513–1515) of Martin Luther* (Leiden: Brill, 1974).

15. Ibid., 162.

16. See for example, Luther's gloss to Psalm 32[33]:7, in *Luther's Works*, vol. 10, ed. Hilton C. Oswald (St. Louis: Concordia, 1974), 156–57.

17. Forell points out "although Luther did not want to make the Church dependent on a definite place or a definite time and a definite person, he did not say that the church exists apart from place and time and that persons do not belong to the church. He merely said that the Church as the Communion of Saints exists because of the gospel and not because of any of her members." Forell, *Reality of the Church*, 67–68.

18. "Although Luther rejects the vertically-directed *caritas* as the mark of the true *fideles*, there is evidence in the *Dictata* that he retains the horizontal dimension of *caritas* as the mark of unity among the *fideles*." See Hendrix, *Ecclesia in Via*, 214.

19. Pauck, *Heritage of the Reformation*, 33.

20. For Luther's understanding of the relationship between word and spirit, see Regin Prenter, *Spiritus Creator*, trans. John M. Jensen (Philadelphia: Muhlenberg, 1953).

21. Lohse, *Martin Luther*, 179.

22. Christoph Schwöbel, "The Creature of the Word: Recovering the Ecclesiology of the Reformers," in *On Being the Church: Essays on the Christian Community*, ed. Colin E. Gunton and Daniel W. Hardy (Edinburgh: T&T Clark, 1989), 131.

23. Martin Luther, "The Large Catechism," in Robert Kolb and Timothy J. Wengert, eds., *The Book of Concord: The Confessions of the Evangelical Lutheran Church*, trans. Charles Arand, et al. (Minneapolis: Fortress Press, 2000), 436.

24. Veli-Matti Kärkkäinen, *An Introduction to Ecclesiology: Ecumenical, Historical, and Global Perspectives* (Downers Grove, IL: InterVarsity, 2002), 40.

25. Dulles, *Models of the Church*, 77.

26. For example, see Karl Barth, *The Church and the Political Problem of Our Day* (New York: Scribners, 1939).

27. Arthur Cochrane, *The Church's Confession under Hitler*, 2d ed., Pittsburgh Reprint Series 4, ed. Dikran Y. Hadidian (Pittsburgh: Pickwick, 1976), 19.

28. Edmund Schlink, "The Witness of the German Lutheran Church Struggle," in *Man's Disorder and God's Design*, vol. I, ed. W. A. Visser't Hooft (New York: Harper & Bros., 1948), 97–98.

29. Ibid., 98–99. Chief among these—which would become the major driving motivation behind the Confessing Church—was the so-called "Aryan paragraph"; see Cochrane, *Church's Confession*, 109.

30. Kent S. Knutson, "The Community of Faith and the Word: An Inquiry into the Concept of the Church in Contemporary Lutheranism," PhD diss., Union Theological Seminary, 1961, 265.

31. Cited in Cochrane, *Church's Confession*, 123–24; italics are Barth's.

32. See Eric G. Jay, *The Church: Its Changing Image Through Twenty Centuries* (Atlanta: John Knox, 1980), 352–53; and E. Lamirande, "Roman Catholic Reactions to Karl Barth's Ecclesiology," *Canadian Journal of Theology* 14, no. 11 (1968): 28–42.

33. Knutson, "Community of Faith," 268–69. See Karl Barth, "The Church—the Living Congregation of the Living Word Jesus Christ," in Visser't Hooft, ed., *Man's Disorder and God's Design*, 67–76.

34. Karl Barth, *Church Dogmatics* IV, Part 1, ed. G. W. Bromiley and T. F. Torrance (Edinburgh: T&T Clark, 1956), 652, his emphasis. Hereafter *CD*.

35. Barth, "The Church," 68.

36. Ibid.

37. For example, Knutson, "Community of Faith," 273, 302.

38. The congregation is Barth's primary referent for the church and is related to his preference for using the German term *Gemeinde* (community) over *Kirche* (church) in writing about ecclesiology. Kimlyn Bender, *Karl Barth's Christological Ecclesiology* (Burlington, VT: Ashgate, 2005), 121.

39. Barth, "The Church," 69. See also *CD* II, Part 1, ed. G. W. Bromiley and T. F. Torrance (Edinburgh: T&T Clark, 1957), 217.

40. Barth, *CD* IV:1, 653. For Barth, this is accomplished by the "awakening power" of the Holy Spirit; *CD* IV:1, 151.

41. Ibid., 151.

42. Bender, *Karl Barth's Christological Ecclesiology*, 153.

43. Ibid., 156–57.

44. Ibid., 102.

45. Ibid., 97.

46. Knutson, "Community of Faith," 272.

47. M. St. Agnes Cunningham, "Bultmann: A Theology of the Word," *Continuum* 4, no. 1 (1966): 40.

48. Gerhard Ebeling, *The Nature of Faith,* trans. Ronald Gregor Smith (Philadelphia: Fortress Press, 1961), 187.

49. Ibid., 95.

50. Ibid., 155.

51. Forde is still arguably "the chief representative of what he called 'radical Lutheranism,' a form of Lutheran confessional theology that tested everything by the chief article on justification and in doing so found much ecumenical and other Lutheran theology to be deficient." Joseph A. Burgess and Marc Kolden, eds., *By Faith Alone: Essays on Justification in Honor of Gerhard O. Forde* (Grand Rapids: Eerdmans, 2004), 7.

52. See Gerhard Forde, "*lex semper accusat?* Nineteenth Century Roots of Our Current Dilemma," *dialog* 9 (1970): 265–74.

53. Ibid., 272.

54. See Gerhard Forde, "Fake Theology: Reflections on Antinomianism Past and Present," *dialog* 22 (1983): 246–51.

55. Gerhard Forde, "Law and Gospel in Luther's Hermeneutic," *Interpretation* 37 (1983): 247.

56. Gerhard Forde, "Law and Gospel as the Methodological Principle of Theology," in *Theological Perspectives: A Discussion of Contemporary Issues in Lutheran Theology by Members of the Department of Religion at Luther College* (Decorah, IA: Luther College Press, 1967), 63.

57. Gerhard Forde, "The Work of Christ," in *Christian Dogmatics*, vol. II, ed. Carl E. Braaten and Robert W. Jenson (Philadelphia: Fortress Press, 1984), 79. Hereafter *ChD.*

58. This is related to the hermeneutical shift described above by Hendrix; in both cases, the active word of God is the orienting principle for Christian life, rather than the "letter" of the text or any other external thing.

59. Forde, "Law and Gospel in Luther's Hermeneutic," 240–52.

60. Proclamation is more specific than preaching, but it is also more comprehensive, as it occurs apart from preaching in the sacraments and mutual conversation of Christians. Gerhard Forde, *Theology Is for Proclamation* (Minneapolis: Fortress Press, 1990), 1.

61. Ibid., 17.

62. Ibid., 31.

63. Ibid.

64. Ibid., 33.

65. Forde, "Work of Christ," 71–72.

66. Ibid., 58.

67. Gerhard Forde, "Does the Gospel Have a Future? Barth's Romans Revisited," *Word & World* 14, no. 1 (1994): 71.

68. Gerhard Forde, "The Christian Life," in *ChD* II: 410–11. Thus for Forde, sanctification is nothing more than "getting used to justification."

69. Forde, *Theology Is for Proclamation*, 186.

70. Ibid., 187.

71. Ibid., 188.

72. Gerhard Forde, "The Meaning of *Satis Est,*" *Lutheran Forum* 26, no. 4 (1992): 17.

73. Gerhard Forde, *Where God Meets Man: Luther's Down-to-Earth Approach to the Gospel* (Minneapolis: Augsburg, 1972), 116–18.

74. Gerhard Forde, "Infallibility Language and the Early Lutheran Tradition," in *Teaching Authority & Infallibility in the Church: Lutherans and Catholics in Dialogue VI*, ed. Paul C. Empie, et al. (Minneapolis: Augsburg, 1978), 132.

75. Ibid., 136; italics his.

76. Forde, *Theology Is For Proclamation*, 188.

77. For example, see Gerhard Forde, "Once More into the Breach: Some Questions about Key 73," *dialog* 12 (1973): 7–14.

78. Michael Horton, *Covenant and Eschatology: The Divine Drama* (Louisville: Westminster John Knox, 2002), 79.

79. Ibid., 70–71.

80. Michael Horton, *People and Place: A Covenant Ecclesiology* (Louisville: Westminster John Knox, 2008), 178.

81. Horton, *Covenant and Eschatology*, 135.

82. Horton draws upon another Reformed theologian, Stephen Webb, who wrote that the Reformation represents "an event within the history of sound," an event of "revocalizing the Word." Horton, *People and Place*, 45.

83. Ibid., 136. Not surprisingly, Horton has more room for human participation in the covenant, in terms of response, and a more positive view of the "third use of the law."

84. Ibid., 177.

85. Ibid., 47.

86. Ibid., 41.

87. Ibid., 39.

88. Ibid., 74.

89. Ibid., 39n3.

90. Ibid., 61.

91. Horton does not see covenantal theology as inimical to the law-gospel hermeneutic, as some Reformed theologians do. See Michael Horton, "Law, Gospel, Covenant: Reassessing some emerging antitheses," *Westminster Theological* Journal 64 (2002): 279–87.

92. Horton, *Covenant and Eschatology*, 204, citing Walter Brueggeman.

93. Ibid., 235.

94. Horton, *People and Place*, x. The "total Christ" is a concept used by the church fathers to refer to the risen Christ including and included in his community. Among those Horton engages are Joseph Ratzinger (who became Pope Benedict XVI) and John Zizioulas, both of whom are "deeply indebted to idealist notions of the 'corporate personality' that finally surrenders the many to the one after all . . . *totus Christus* now understood as a single (corporate) person more than as a communion of saints." Ibid., 164–65).

95. Ibid., 33.

96. He is equally critical of free-church ecclesiologies that have a more contractual view of the church; instead of being a the creation of the word, the church becomes "a creation of the market." Ibid., 180.

97. Ibid., 195.

98. Ibid., 203.

99. Ibid.

100. Ibid., 231.

101. Ibid., 254–55.

102. Ibid., 251. As I show in ch. 4, I do not think this is a fair critique of the *missio Dei* paradigm.

103. Forde, *Theology Is for Proclamation*, 190.

104. See also Steven D. Paulson, "Do Lutherans Need a New Ecclesiology?" *Lutheran Quarterly* 15 (2001): 217–34.

105. I thank Christian Scharen for this insight.

3

The Church as Communion

The second paradigm, communion ecclesiology, offers another theological answer to the question of the church's identity. This paradigm locates the being of the church not in an "event" but in the very divine life of the Triune God. Although communion ecclesiology does not come to the fore as a central ecclesiological concept in Western theology until the twentieth century, it has biblical origins and is associated with the Holy Spirit, as seen in the Pauline greeting: "the grace of our Lord Jesus Christ, the love of God, and the communion [*koinonia*] of the Holy Spirit" (2 Cor. 13:13). Communion ecclesiology draws on the twofold biblical meaning of *koinonia*: fellowship and a common participation or sharing in something, in this case, salvation in Christ. Theologically, *koinonia* is defined as a gift of God with vertical and horizontal aspects: believers are drawn into communion with the Triune God and with one another through their incorporation into the body of Christ, which happens through Baptism and Eucharist. The most dominant version grounds the communion of the church in the perichoretic communion of the persons of the Trinity.[1]

THE EMERGENCE OF COMMUNION ECCLESIOLOGY IN TWENTIETH-CENTURY ROMAN CATHOLICISM

Communion ecclesiology emerged in the twentieth century as a response to questions of ecclesial self-understanding in Roman Catholic, Orthodox, and Protestant churches. It has been deemed by Josephs Cardinal Ratzinger as "the basic ecclesiology" and is becoming the major paradigm for ecumenical ecclesiology.

Leading up to the Second Vatican Council, theologians, most notably Yves Congar, rediscovered the concept of communion as a fuller way of speaking about the nature of the church that goes beyond the hierarchical and clerical.

Before Vatican II, ecclesiology was dominated by neoscholastic theologians who viewed the church primarily in christological terms and defined the church in juridical categories as a hierarchical society.[2] The 1940s saw a return to the patristic sources and a retrieval of the mystical-body theology as a response to the growing dissatisfaction with neoscholasticism. This paved the way for Pope Pius XII to publish the 1943 encyclical *Mystici corporis Christi* ("The Mystical Body of Christ"), the most comprehensive official Catholic pronouncement on the church prior to Vatican II. In this encyclical, Pius stresses the necessity of the church's visibility as the body of Christ and, in its most memorable passage, affirms that "the Mystical Body is identical with the Roman Catholic Church."[3]

This same period saw other theological contributions from the "ressourcement [return to the sources] movement," in particular that of Congar, who is regarded as the most influential ecclesiologist between *Mystici corporis* and Vatican II. Congar sought to reclaim the experience of the church in its first millennium, before its domination in society and culture, as a resource for contemporary ecclesiology. His work also reflected a shift from a christocentric to a more trinitarian method. Congar's theological reflection on the central biblical and trinitarian images of the church—people of God, body of Christ, and temple of the Holy Spirit—brought fresh new perspectives to the discussion. For Congar, the central point of Paul's body-of-Christ motif was not, as many had argued in the decades leading up to Vatican II, an insistence on institutional visibility, but an affirmation of unity in plurality. Congar's own preference seemed to be for the image "temple of the Spirit," which, according to Avery Dulles, "suggested the dimensions of interiority and spirituality, giving rise to an ecclesiology of communion. In contrast to . . . [emphasizing] the visible structures of the Church, Congar looked upon the institutional structures as mere means . . . preferring to define the Church essentially as a community in the Spirit, a *congregatio fidelium*."[4] As the people of God, laypersons should not be viewed only as recipients of the ministry of priests and bishops, but as active and responsible subjects called to transform the world with the light of the gospel.[5] His long-held ecumenical concerns also shaped his ecclesiology, which would in turn influence the council in significant ways. Already in 1939 he spoke of Protestants as separated brethren and posited that, because there are salvific elements in them, one may recognize degrees of communion with other Christians.

The Second Vatican Council

The ecclesiology of Vatican II generally followed the ressourcement theology rather than neoscholasticism, but "made no sharp break with the official teaching of the recent past. The shift was one of emphasis more than substance, of rhetoric more than doctrine."[6] The Vatican II documents integrate the concept of the church as the body of Christ and the church as the people of God into what the 1985 Synod of Bishops would declare is "a central and fundamental" idea to emerge from the council: an ecclesiology of *koinonia* or communion.[7] The communion concept is seen as involving diversity in unity, the spirit of collegiality, and participation and co-responsibility at every level of the church. Communion ecclesiology draws on and builds on the notion of the church as a people of God, for the church is manifested in "the full and active participation of all God's holy people" and the church of Christ is really present "in all legitimately organized groups of the faithful."[8] Communion ecclesiology also retrieves a biblical and patristic idea of the whole Christ, *totus Christus*, by which all of humanity are not only joined to the body of Christ through grace in a covenant with Christ the head, but participate in Christ in such manner as to form a single being.[9] This paradigm avoids the difficulties of the older mystical-body theology—in particular, "naïve identification" between Christ and the church, where the church is seen as a prolongation of the incarnation and can easily become triumphalist—by introducing the mediating category of "sacrament" and giving communion a more explicit trinitarian foundation.[10]

The primary emphasis in all communion ecclesiologies is on relationship to Christ and sacramental incorporation into the Triune God, rather than organizational structures or community. For Susan Wood and others, "Ecclesial communion is modeled on the communion of *perichoresis* of the Father, Son, and Spirit in their Trinitarian relationship," whereby the persons maintain distinctive identities, but through mutual interpenetration (*perichoresis*), share a unity of being and will. Christians are "actually caught up in the dynamic interrelationship of Father, Son, and Spirit" by virtue of their incorporation into the body of Christ and participation in Christ.[11] The communion of members in the church is compared to and grounded in the communion of divine persons within the Trinity.[12] The Eucharist is not only the visible sign of communion in and with Christ; it is constitutive of ecclesial communion, "for in partaking one bread, we become one body." In other words, "For where the Eucharist is, there is the church."[13] Eucharist is the culmination and visible expression of the communion begun by incorporation into the body of Christ through Baptism. According to Wood, the mission of the church in this model is best described as reconciliation, "extending the concept from one of juridical penance and repentance for sin to one of incorporation into the body. The dominant metaphor for sin becomes alienation and isolation from the body of Christ, and the metaphor for grace is communion with the body."[14]

Communion ecclesiology gives special attention to the local or particular church without denying the importance of hierarchical communion with the pope. It is important for Protestants to understand that in Catholic (as well as Orthodox) understanding, a "local church" is a diocese, not a congregation. A local or particular church is defined by the presence not only of the Eucharist but also a bishop, who through his office links the church with other eucharistic communities.[15] The local church is not a subdivision of the universal church but relates to the universal church (and other local churches) through the celebration of the Eucharist by the bishop. The universal church is defined in eucharistic terms as well. "The universal church subsists in, but is not limited to, each particular church in an analogous way to which Christ is entirely present in, but it not limited to, each eucharistic celebration."[16] Each particular church in this way is "wholly church," but no particular church can be the whole church in isolation from other local churches. Another way to say this is that the local church is the particular, concrete place where the universal church is found.[17] In spite of the new attention given to the local church, however, an often-polarizing tension remains between those Catholics who emphasize the priority of the universal church (the dominant position prior to Vatican II) and those who emphasize the priority of the local church.[18]

Communion ecclesiology also offers a way to address the division of the churches. The term occurs frequently in the Decree on Ecumenism (one of the documents of Vatican II) and has proven fruitful in ecumenical dialogues because communion is a more "elastic concept than church membership" as it admits degrees of unity and distinctions such as full or partial communion.[19] At the same time, the greatest agreement on what communion means lies in the mutual acceptance of the invisible elements of *koinonia* as described in the Scriptures,[20] such as the nature of the church as *koinonia* or communion, ecclesial communion being grounded in trinitarian communion, the Holy Spirit as the source of communion, and the communion Christians have with each other as the result of communion with the Triune God. The difficulty comes more with the visible elements of communion: common profession of faith, sacraments, and especially mutually recognized (and thereby interchangeable) ministry.[21] All Christian traditions affirm the centrality and presence of communion in their traditions, but the visible forms that communion takes will vary, especially with regard to the structures of communion. For Roman Catholics, of course, full communion requires some understanding not only of the role of episcopacy in establishing and representing ecclesial *koinonia*, but also that of papal primacy.[22] In contrast, the Lutheran World Federation adopted the concept of communion for its self-definition without adopting a particular form of polity or structure for the church.[23] While affirming the trinitarian foundation of ecclesial communion, the statement does not focus on the structure or forms of how that communion is lived out and realized.

THE QUEST FOR THE UNITY OF THE CHURCH IN THE MODERN ECUMENICAL MOVEMENT

Roman Catholics were not the only ones wrestling with ecclesiology in the mid-twentieth century. With the modern ecumenical movement in full sway, Protestants increasingly concerned themselves with the question of the Christian unity and, therefore, the nature of the church, thus introducing a significant shift in ecumenical method at this time. Previously, ecumenical dialogue followed a comparative method that one began by using one's own ecclesial tradition. Ecumenists were beginning to realize the limitations of this method and at the Third World Faith and Order Conference in Lund (1952) proposed a new christological method as a means of breaking through ecclesial divisions.[24] Anders Nygren, a conference participant, stated, "Instead of taking the different views of the various communions as our point of departure, we must instead take Christ, who is himself the unity of the Church. In other words, we must consider the Church's Christological basis, the Church as 'the Body of Christ.'"[25] Consequently, the unity of the church in Christ is a given and must be the starting point for ecumenism. This means that Christians do not effect or actualize unity; rather, they are called to bring that unity to full expression. This has consequences for the goal of the ecumenical movement. When one begins with the givenness of the church's unity, rather than beginning with the diversity among Christian communions, the question of the church's organization is of secondary importance. The new goal is for different denominations to acknowledge one another fully as members of the one body of Christ and to make that unity visible by sharing the Lord's Supper together.

Protestant theologians found themselves focusing anew on the Pauline metaphor of the body of Christ and, in particular, searching for ways to understand the relationship *between* Christ and the church without strictly identifying them. They especially were concerned to avoid any notion of the pre–Vatican II Catholic understanding of the church as Christ's mystical body, and especially the concept of the church as the "extension of the incarnation" or "ongoing incarnation." The dangers of this view are addressed by a number of Protestant authors in the mid-twentieth century.[26] First, by identifying ecclesiology with Christology, such a concept of the church seems to challenge the unique and complete nature of Christ's incarnation. As Lesslie Newbigin states, ". . . Christ's presence with His Church since Pentecost is in a different manner from His presence on earth 'in the days of flesh.'"[27] It also implies that Christ loses his identity in and is somehow contained by the church. J. Robert Nelson argues that if the church is truly the continuation of Christ's incarnation, "there is no need for it to point beyond itself to Christ—as true preaching must do."[28]

With these concerns in mind, Nygren's colleague, Gustaf Aulén, proposed that the term "body of Christ" emphasizes the unity between Christ and the church more than any other New Testament image (for instance, vine and branches, temple) and this "is not a question of identity but of a relationship. The church is not coterminous with Christ. . . . The church cannot take the place of Christ or function as an intermediary between Christ and humanity."[29] Rather, the term "body of Christ" suggests the inseparable unity between Christ and his body, meaning that the church exists in and through Christ, and Christ cannot be conceived of without his church. This christological focus would turn out to be the first step toward a fully trinitarian method in the ecumenical moment's ecclesiology, as recognized by the next World Council of Churches (WCC) meeting in Montreal (1963).[30] This trinitarian reference becomes more explicit as the *koinonia*/communion paradigm becomes more prominent in the work of the WCC and other church bodies.[31]

THE COMMUNION PARADIGM
IN THE MODERN ECUMENICAL MOVEMENT

Because of its biblical basis and emphasis on participation as union with God and one another, communion ecclesiology has been promoted by many ecumenists as a promising concept for facilitating Christian unity.[32] The concept is able to bring together and integrate various elements of ecclesiology that are often in tension with each other: divine/human, vertical/horizontal, local/universal, and unity/diversity. Its trinitarian foundation offers a deeper theological and spiritual vision for the church than related terms such as "community" or fellowship" while still responding to the contemporary longing for greater community in church and society. The communion of the churches is a sign for the communion God wishes ultimately to have with all of humankind. Finally, it enables a way to envision visible unity that avoids negative associations, for example, that unity means uniformity or undifferentiated homogenization, or a unity based on the "lowest common denominator."[33]

Though not yet as dominant as in Roman Catholicism, the concept of *koinonia* or communion has become a key perspective in the work of the Faith and Order Commission of the World Council of Churches[34] and bilateral dialogues. This includes the 1994 Lutheran–Roman Catholic International Dialogue on the "Church and Justification,"[35] which has a lengthy section on the church as communion that emphasizes the trinitarian foundation of the church and a shared, common witness on the meaning of "communion" as openness to other local churches (in spite of the recognition that differences remain on how both traditions define "local church").[36]

Communion also has become the central concept in the ecclesial self-understanding of both the Lutheran World Federation (LWF) and the World Communion of Reformed Churches (WCRC). In 1990, the Eighth Assembly of the LWF voted to change its constitution to define the LWF as a "communion of churches which confess the triune God, agree in the proclamation of the Word, and are united in pulpit and altar fellowship."[37] A study was commissioned to respond to concerns raised over the meaning of communion and the implications for its structural expression,[38] resulting in the 1997 statement "Toward a Lutheran Understanding of Communion."[39] This document affirms that the foundation of communion in the church is the communion of the divine life: the Triune God's own self-giving nature and action through word and sacrament. The church's nature and mission are drawn from an understanding of God's being as a communion of persons. Communion is described as a process of greater and deeper unity in both the ecclesial and broader human community that reflects the perichoretic union of the persons of the Trinity. The document calls the church to live in accordance with the gift of communion, which includes finding ways to witness to and express more visibly the communion that already exists among Christians. Communion includes deepening understanding, mutual recognition and sharing between distinct "others" (for example, ecclesial traditions, socioeconomic and racial groups) and the spiritual and material gifts that each member or group brings. As a communion, the church is called to proclaim to a "threatened and broken world in word and deed, through the witness of its life that God's salvation, hope, and reconciliation have come into our midst in the life, death, and resurrection of Jesus Christ."[40] Little is said about the forms and structures of communion (for instance, episcopacy) except to stress that that these are not foundational to a Lutheran understanding of the church.

In 2010 World Alliance of Reformed Churches (WARC) and the Reformed Ecumenical Council (REC) united to form the World Communion of Reformed Churches. The word *communion* in the new organization's name is significant. At its last meeting in Trinidad, the Executive Committee of WARC offered the following definition:

> Communion is an expression of our being together in the body of Christ as we move toward that oneness which is the gift and calling of God, fully expressed in the Trinity. Our desire to enter into communion signifies the commitment of our churches, in the richness of our diversity, to mutual caring, respect and service of one another, as witness to our common calling by the Spirit of God in Jesus Christ.[41]

The new name signals a shift similar to that of the LWF, but Douwe Visser wishes that the Reformed had followed a process more like the LWF, particularly, that there would have been more theological reflection, specifically from the Reformed tradition, about the meaning of communion. The draft constitution of WCRC "defines 'communion' in a theologically, but not after a process of theological reflection and consultation."[42] Neither is there any reflection on how the WCRC will function as a "communion."

Although communion has been explored as an ecclesiological concept in various ecumenical dialogues and by global church bodies such as the LWF and WARC, it is an unfortunate fact that many Protestant theologians remain woefully unaware of these contributions. In light of this, it is all the more striking that the communion paradigm has recently been embraced by North American theologians with Reformation roots.[43]

ROBERT W. JENSON'S ONTIC-COMMUNION ECCLESIOLOGY

Robert W. Jenson offers perhaps the fullest engagement with communion ecclesiology of any individual Lutheran theologian. His concern with the unity and catholicity of the church leads him to posit a strongly christological (though trinitarian) and ontological ecclesiology. His theology is unapologetically ecumenical in its vision and dialogue partners, as he draws not only on Martin Luther but on the broader tradition of the church, including the Cappadocians, Augustine, Thomas Aquinas, Karl Barth, Vatican II, as well as contemporary theologians from the Catholic and Orthodox traditions.

Throughout his career, Jenson has grounded his theological project in the categories of story and promise. Jenson places these categories against the backdrop of the great Reformation insight that God's grace occurs as word, as the address by which one person communicates him- or herself to another. For God's word to be grace, "this speaking must itself be gratuitous in its linguistic character. The kind of speaking that bestows something *gratis* can be specified: it is promising that it does so."[44] Drawing on the traditional Lutheran distinction between law and gospel (promise), Jenson defines promise eschatologically in contrast to law: the law posits the future as obligation whereas promise posits it as gift. The gospel is God's promise because it opens a future unconditionally.

For a promise to mean anything, however, depends on the one who is making it. Thus Jenson's two poles of story and promise are integrally related to his central theological concern: the identity of God. For Jenson, the word "'God,' whatever else it may be good for, can carry no cognitive freight. One must ask and answer the question of God's *identity*: Who are we talking about when we say "God"?[45] God's self-identification as the God of unconditional promise is worked out through the particular narrative history of Israel and Jesus Christ, the culmination of which is his death and resurrection.[46] The narrative—summarized in the gospel sentence, "Jesus is risen"—identifies the one who is proclaimed as final future.[47] This necessarily leads to the doctrine of the Trinity, which functions to give us God's identity. The phrase "Father, Son, and Holy Spirit" is for Jenson "a compressed telling of the total narrative by which Scripture identifies God and a personal name for God so specified in it."[48] Further, while Jenson follows Barth in calling God "event,"[49] in his trinitarian theology he emphasizes relationality as being at the heart of who God is. For Jenson, God's "being" subsists in the relations of the three persons or, as he prefers, "identifies:"[50] Father, Son, and Holy Spirit. To affirm that the Son, though distinct from the Father, is, "internally related to the Father," in "a relation necessary to his being God," is to affirm nothing less than *To be God is to be related.*"[51]

If God is identified with the narrative of Israel and Jesus Christ, then it is through the drama of these events that God is known. Since human beings know God in God's address to us, an address that comes in the form of a promise secured by God's identity, we can say that to be human means to be created by and to respond to God's promise.[52] The content of this promise is God's own self—not as a substance or "being," on the one hand, nor as "act" or "word-event," on the other—but as a narrated history with which God is identified, a history that anticipates the fulfillment of the promise. Because God is communicating God's own self, this word makes one righteous as it pronounces one righteous.[53] Faith unites the soul to Christ in a happy exchange, and by this participation in Christ, the faithful are ontically righteous, meaning that the believer has Christ's righteousness. In contrast to Gerhard Forde, Jenson describes the new life in moral terms since righteousness is possible in Christ; however, he is no more optimistic than Forde about moral progress in this life. "Short of the End, the believer never advances beyond his or her baptism, but instead falls behind it and must catch up to it."[54] In the present, the believer only lives "by *return*—by ever hearing the promise."[55]

Unlike the traditional Protestant view, Jenson wishes to consider the church not *primarily* as "a creature of the gospel," but "in its own proper entity, in which it is in God's intention antecedent to the gospel."[56] Jenson asserts that "the church finds its model, its origin and its end in the mystery of the one God in three persons."[57] The church has its origin not only in the Christ event as narrated in the Gospels;[58] the church also originates by the will of the Father, who predestines the church in the Son. That is, the one sole object of eternal election is Jesus with his people, the *totus Christus*.[59]

Though predestined with Christ, the church is not the fulfillment of God's promises to Israel, but an eschatological detour created by the delay of the parousia.[60] Neither a realization of the new age nor a this-worldly entity only, the church is "precisely an event *within the event* of the new age's advent." The church is not the kingdom of God, but its being is grounded in this eschatological reality, which enables it to carry the sacramental presence of the kingdom within it.[61] The Holy Spirit is the eschatological reality of God and the freedom that occurs in the relations between the triune identities. The Spirit who frees the Father for the Son (and vice versa) is also "the one who frees the Christian community" for God and for the world.[62] In other words, the work of the Spirit is to unite the Head with the body of Christ.[63] The same Spirit poured out at Pentecost also frees the church to become a prophetic community, through whom the story continues to be told in proclamation and praise.[64]

For Jenson, "people of God," "body of Christ," and "temple of the Spirit" are not images from which to pick and choose but, rather, ontic realities that must be seen together. Even though "people of God" is the central category in *Lumen Gentium*, Jenson suggests constraint in its appropriation because nearly all mentions of the "people of God" in the New Testament refer to Israel.[65] The few clear New Testament references to the church as the people of God are eschatological.[66] The mark of this eschatological community is the sacrament of Baptism, which leads to the second image, "temple of the Spirit," because, as Jenson states, "the sacramental efficacy of baptism is that it irrevocably initiates into the church and that the spirit of the church is the Holy Spirit himself."[67] Jenson brings these two images together in a third concept, that of "polity." He affirms that it is the Holy Spirit's proper work to make the church, and "the Spirit does this by giving himself to be the spirit of this community, by bestowing his own eschatological power to be her liveliness."[68] By the Spirit, Jenson means the Spirit of prophecy of the scriptural narrative, in both Old and New Testaments. The narrative of Pentecost shows that prophecy is a gift given to the whole church, making the church as a whole a prophesying community or "a single communal prophet."[69] Rather than drawing on the biblical narrative at this point, he turns instead to Augustine's definition of polity as "a people united in a common spirit, that is, a people who have become a community."[70]

Jenson brings the concept of "polity" together with that of "body of Christ" into his central ecclesiological concept, which is *communion.* The "body of Christ" for Paul is not a metaphor for the church. The church is "ontologically the risen body of Christ."[71] For Paul, a person's embodiment is her availability to another person. A body that is not embodied is not good news to anyone. It follows from the gospel profession, "Jesus is risen," that Jesus has a body, which means that his body must be someplace. "That someplace is on the altar of the Eucharist."[72] The church is the body of Christ, because through the church, Christ is made personally and bodily available to its own members and to the world. Central to Jenson's thinking here is the insight that churchly and eucharistic communion *both* are communion in the body of Christ. According to Jenson, the Eucharist promises that "*there* is my body in the world, and you here eating and drinking commune in it. It promises: *there* is the actual historical church and you are she."[73]

Jenson affirms that "the *communio*-doctrine of the church's being is in part christological and eucharistic,"[74] and rooted in the communion within the Triune God. It is not enough to say that Christians have communion with one another because individually they have the same communion with Christ. Jenson goes on to explore what it means for the church's structure to be drawn from the nature of the church as communion, rather than from secular models. That means that "any level or organ of ecclesial actuality that can truly be called church must itself be constituted as communion" and "these communions are in perichoretic communion with each other."[75] Because this communion or fellowship is founded in the one Triune God, there can only be one such fellowship. Since this body cannot meet face to face until the end, in the meantime each local fellowship recognizes one another in the common practice of fellowship, the central act of which is the celebration of the Eucharist. For Jenson, a threefold hierarchical office of ministry ensures the church a continuity of identity and authority through sacrament and doctrine. However, leaders must serve the whole people of God in humility, "not in an exercise *of* dominion of the church but 'a primacy of love' *within* the church. In other words, the hierarchy must itself reflect the nature of the church's communion."[76]

For Jenson, the church's mission is to find a way to speak the gospel in light of the problems posed by postmodernity: specifically, that we no longer live in a narratable world in which promises are made and kept. Jenson proposes that the church's mission in this context is that the church *be* that "world," a communion in which authentic promises are made and kept whereby God's will is followed through its dramatic enactment God's truth in the liturgy, the center of which is the celebration of Eucharist.[77]

PHILIP BUTIN'S TRINITARIAN ECCLESIOLOGY

A fully developed communion ecclesiology has yet to appear from a single Reformed theologian, although several Reformed theologians have positively engaged the concept, albeit with some caution.[78] Philip Butin's reclamation of Calvin's trinitarian theology as the key to his theology and ecclesiology provides the strongest foundation for a Reformed communion ecclesiology.[79] Butin notes the importance of context for the task of ecclesiology. He points to the radical shift taking place with regard to the cultural role of the mainline churches in the United States, which has led to an "identity crisis" within mainstream Protestantism, "not the least within its Reformation traditions."[80] The mainline churches have become culturally disestablished and marginalized as society has become increasingly pluralistic and diverse. This has led to two related effects: an increase in the number of unchurched persons but also a culturally disintegrating effect brought about by pluralism and a decrease in shared cultural values. Further, the idea of the autonomous self in the West has led to what may be the great crisis of Western culture: "a crisis of relationship."[81] To address these crises theologically, Butin draws on the emerging ecumenical consensus regarding the trinitarian character of God.[82] Echoing Jenson, he writes that "the doctrine of the Trinity teaches us that God is essentially relational" and if human beings are created in God's image, then we are also created for relationship. God intends the divine *koinonia* to be reflected in human *koinonia*.[83] To help the church to reclaim its identity as a community of true *koinonia* and an agent of cultural transformation, Butin turns to John Calvin who defines the church as "a visible embodiment, enactment, and reflection of the Trinitarian grace of God in the world."[84]

Butin argues that the doctrine of the Trinity—rather than God's address to humanity in the word—provides the key to Calvin's theology and ecclesiology. Calvin generally shied away from making claims about what contemporary theologians call "the immanent Trinity" (that is, God in God's own eternal being), preferring to emphasize the external, economic work of the Trinity, because the divine-human relationship is in the arena of the economy of salvation.[85] However, his reading of John's Gospel led him to affirm a perichoretic model of relations between the three persons of the Trinity.[86] Specifically, he explored the idea that the Father is not only the revealer, but the one who is revealed. What we can know about the Father we know through the Son (the Word), by the power of the Spirit. Indeed, preaching becomes the word of God by the perichoretically interactive operation of the immanent Trinity and is thus revelatory of God's being.[87]

For Calvin, the Trinity also constitutes the pattern of the divine-human relationship in the realm of redemption, though with a clear christological focus. Calvin's Christology centers on Christ's work of mediation, which "establishes a 'mutual conjunction' whereby the divinity of Christ and our human nature are made to 'coalesce with each other,' such that God is able to 'dwell with us'" through the Holy Spirit's operation in believers.[88] In the first place, redemption includes reconciliation of human beings—alienated from God by sin—to God. Because salvation in no way can depend on human merit, Calvin and later Reformed theology emphasizes the free election of persons to redemption by the will of the Father.[89] For Calvin, redemption also includes restoration of the divine image in human beings. Butin argues that Calvin's entire doctrine of the Christian life stands under the theme of the trinitarian restoration of the divine image in Christ. Justification and sanctification are the two moments in the restoration of the divine image that depend on the gracious will and election of the Father, the mediation of the Son, and the illumination of the Holy Spirit. Faith brings believers into union with Christ, by which they are justified, sin is overcome, and the divine image restored. Although faith is the work of the Holy Spirit, "faith is a divinely given receptivity to what the triune God shows us of God's own self,"[90] making this, too, an act of the whole

Trinity.[91] In a similar way, Calvin attributes sanctification, the event by which "authentic human response can be graciously constituted and reoriented toward the Triune God," to the whole Trinity.[92]

Calvin viewed the church (and sacraments as the means of grace) also in terms of the perichoretic action of the one God. The Triune God instituted the church—a specific, visible, corporeal human community—"to be the normative context within and through which to communicate divine grace to us"[93] and which its members thereby might embody in their life together. Butin states, "Because God exists in the eternal *koinonia* of Father, Son, and Holy Spirit, human *koinonia* begins in, depends on, and grows out of our living relationship with the triune God," a relationship that is "cultivated, maintained, and nourished" by prayer and worship.[94] Calvin's answer to the Reformation question "Where is the true church?" echoes that given by the Lutheran Reformers. Worship is the event in which the visible community of believers is most authentically the church because that is where the Triune God communicates divine grace to the faithful through word and sacrament. Worship is not primarily something we offer to God but is "gracious participation in the triune God's own life and *koinonia*."[95] This *koinonia* is the work of the Holy Spirit who unites us to the Son in his unbroken communion with the Father. Calvin expresses the corporate life of the church in trinitarian terms. The church is the matrix in which the triune grace of God is seen in and communicated to human beings.[96]

Although the word remains the primary mark of the church for Calvin (as for Luther), Butin argues that it is in the Eucharist where "the coherence of Calvin's Trinitarian paradigm for the divine-human relationship comes to its most concentrated and distinguishing visible expression."[97] Calvin's primary theological concern with the Eucharist is not how Christ is present in the elements of wine and bread; "rather, it was how God worked in the Eucharist to unite believers to Christ by the Spirit, and the benefits that this union brought."[98] The Eucharist acts as a "mirror" that reveals trinitarian grace to us in Christ, but it also "maintains and enhances the believers' actual communion with Christ "through its provision of spiritual nourishment."[99] Calvin draws an intimate connection between the flesh of Christ in the Eucharist and the church itself, Christ's body in its fullness.[100] The great mystery of the Eucharist is the "coherence of the divine-human relationship through the believers' union with Christ, which is sealed by the Holy Spirit as the bond of that union."[101]

Calvin's sense of the trinitarian grounding of the church's being in divine election is the basis of his consistent appeal to Christ's sole headship as the fundamental principle of church order, leading him to a more dynamic and interactive (rather than hierarchical) polity.[102] Because the church's ministry is Christ's ministry, it means that the ministry believers enact is always Christ's and that the pattern for the church's ministry is the threefold ministry of Christ.[103] The church exercises its royal ministry by recognizing Christ as its only king and head and resisting hierarchical views of church structure that focus power in the ordained ministry or other official church leaders.[104] The church exercises its priestly ministry by helping people find the reconciliation and healing in the gospel, particularly in light of the brokenness experienced by many in society. The church exercises its prophetic ministry by speaking the gospel to those who do not yet hear it.[105]

Butin also draws on pneumatology to articulate a vision of the church's mission as the external breathing-forth of the Spirit within God's own trinitarian life being extended "outside of God to us."[106] Although the church should be the primary context where people are invited and enabled to reflect God's own essential relationality, many people retreat into individual spiritual practices or substitute other human communities.[107] By modeling trinitarian *koinonia* in worship and congregational life, a Christian community can become a sign of God's love to the world. As the goal of mission is the participation of all creation in the *koinonia* of God's own trinitarian life, the privilege of participating in this *koinonia* is not the church's to hoard; it should be shared in the exercise of the church's ministry.

An Assessment of Contemporary Communion Ecclesiologies

The question of the church's being is more central here than in the first paradigm, even though the answer is articulated in terms of a relational, rather than a substance, ontology. The question of the church's unity is closely related. Because of its emphasis on participation as union with God and one another, communion ecclesiology has been heralded by its proponents as a promising ecclesiological concept for enabling Christian unity and for addressing the "crisis of relationship" facing the churches today. This approach locates the identity and unity of the church not primarily in the activity of proclaiming and hearing the promise but in the relationality of the Triune God made concrete through the sacramental presence of Christ in the celebration of the Eucharist. By defining personhood (divine and human) in terms of relationship and communion, communion ecclesiology offers a clear challenge to the individualism of modernity and moves beyond the existential focus of some word-event ecclesiologies.

For both Butin and Jenson, the church is less a "creature of the Word" than a communion of persons called to reflect the divine communion within the Trinity, although both are careful not to begin with the immanent Trinity. Even though Jenson and Butin remain "sons of the Reformation" by emphasizing the revelatory aspect of the gospel (and the importance of personal faith), they see proclamation and hearing of the gospel in word and sacrament as that which brings the believer into perichoretic communion with God. This paradigm keeps relationality central not only to who God is, but also to whom the church is called to be. The divine communion is embodied by the church in its ministry to the world, whether by Jenson's moral, liturgical drama or Butin's more missional enactment of outward love. The church reflects and enables the union God wishes to have with all people. Mission is also defined in terms of unity and reconciliation. Thus communion ecclesiology addresses the question of the church's identity and mission in terms of relationship and reconciliation, offering a robust sense of the church as a *koinonia* of God's love.

Some forms of communion ecclesiology raise concerns and cautions, especially if coupled with "a realized eschatology in which communion with the triune God is understood to be the ever-present reality at the heart of the church's being, albeit sometimes obscured by our failure to be fully in communion with one another." Nicholas Healy warns of a "more or less idealized account of the church that is too readily open to ideological and theological distortion."[108] In some Catholic communion ecclesiologies, the ideal of unity within the body of Christ can and has led the church to focus on its internal life and develop hierarchical structures to ensure unity, and appealing to unity to suppress disagreements and movements calling for change.[109] When "communion" becomes a "closed, static reality," it can "embody oppressive realities of power."[110] We see a difference here between Jenson and Butin, with Jenson being much more amenable to hierarchical structures of communion, perhaps due to his reading of the cultural context as having lost its moral moorings.

Roman Catholic theologian Neil Ormerod admires the attempt to link ecclesiology to the Trinity by means of *communio* and *perichoresis*, but he also finds it problematic because "the divine unity is where God is most different from God's creatures, even the creation that we call church."[111] While we can speak of the church in terms of a "communion of persons" analogously to the Trinity as a "communion of persons," a great difference remains, in that the divine life of the Triune God is without sin while the church is, in the present at least, *simul iustus et peccator* (simultaneously justified and sinful). Both Jenson and Butin avoid this trap; in particular, we saw Butin ground ecclesial communion in trinitarian *perichoresis* in a way that does not skirt the problem of sin or idealize the church. Nonetheless, the problem of sin in the church is not always forthrightly addressed in ecumenical documents that ground the church's nature in the perichoretic communion of the Trinity. In these documents, the focus of our communion with God and one another is to reconcile differences and divisions, without always acknowledging the role that forgiveness of sins plays in the process of reconciliation (both in the human-divine relationship as well as in human-human relationships).[112] An understanding of the church as communion that neglects this aspect of reconciliation is in danger of becoming an idealized concept that can too easily become disconnected from the experience of actual ecclesial communities, which will always find themselves in need of forgiveness and healing. It raises the question as to whether *perichoresis* provides the best foundation for an ecclesial communion that includes reconciliation not only of diversity and differences, but also of sin and broken relationships.[113]

As helpful as the communion paradigm may be for the ecumenical task of reconciling differences between churches, it remains to be seen whether it can be as helpful in a post-Christendom context where the unity of the church is not the primary question being asked. Although in much communion ecclesiology unity is definitive of the church's mission, in that the church is called to be a sign of the unity God wishes to have with all people, Jenson, at least, seems to be more concerned with the body of Christ in worship than out in the world. Jenson recognizes that we have entered into a post-Christendom age in which a "narratable world" can no longer be assumed, which for him means that the church must become that narratable world through the drama of the liturgy. He insists that the church as eucharistic community is not a sectarian community, content to let the world "go to hell." The single most important thing the church can do for the world today (and always) is to intercede for it, in particular to intercede for a rebirth in civic society and polity (a new Christendom?).[114] However, it is unclear how this drama becomes known outside the four walls of a congregation in terms of an outward and witnessing movement to the world,[115] or how this communion lives out its identity as the body of Christ apart from the altar.

Butin is much better on this count, both on mission and on the role of the Spirit, which for Jenson seems also to be limited to the liturgy in the *epiclesis*, the invocation of the Holy Spirit over the elements of bread and wine in the eucharistic prayer. Indeed, Butin's understanding of communion is more centrifugal, opening the church to mission in the world. As Butin writes, "The gracious privilege of participating in the *koinonia* of God's trinitarian life cannot be possessed or kept by the church."[116] God has willed that God's own life would be extended to the world in two missions: the sending of the Son in the incarnation and the sending of the Holy Spirit at the Pentecost, the latter both a parallel and extension of the former. Through the "external breathing-forth of the Spirit within God's own trinitarian life,"[117] all that God has done for humanity in the life, death, and resurrection of Jesus Christ becomes incorporated into the human story through the threefold ministry of the church (priestly, royal, and prophetic). Butin explicitly echoes the language of the *missio Dei* paradigm (which will be treated below) when he writes that "the church's sending forth in mission is actually a participation in the trinitarian mission of God as Son and Spirit, the mission in which God graciously invites the whole creation of God into the loving embrace of God's own trinitarian life."[118] While Butin has yet to develop these ideas into a full ecclesiology, his weaving together of the strengths of both the communion and missional paradigms offers a promising way forward, one that resonates very much with this project.

FOR REFLECTION AND DISCUSSION

1. The concept of the church as "communion" will be new to many Protestant readers. How did the concept of the church as a "communion" emerge in twentieth-century Roman Catholicism? What are some of the central elements of the communion paradigm?

2. Why do both Roman Catholic and Protestant ecumenists see this paradigm as promising for addressing the division of the churches?

3. How do Robert Jenson and Philip Butin develop the communion paradigm from and for their respective traditions (Lutheran and Reformed)? What similarities and differences do you see in these authors, especially with regard to the identity and purpose/mission of the church?

4. What deficits in the word-event paradigm might be addressed by the communion paradigm?

5. What are the contributions of the communion paradigm to the ecclesiological discussion today? How does starting with the communion of the three persons of the Trinity help you think differently about the identity and purpose of the church in today's context? What elements of this paradigm should be retained for a contemporary ecclesiology for post-Christendom age? How would your congregation respond to the ideas in this paradigm?

6. What are the weaknesses of this paradigm? Does it sufficiently address the challenges of the post-Christendom context in which the church finds itself? Why or why not?

Notes

1. Orthodox theologian John Zizioulas's influence is seen in the dominant version; see his *Being as Communion* (Crestwood, NY: St. Vladimir's Seminary Press, 1985). Other communion ecclesiologies start "from below" with the experience of communion with others and with God, rather than the perichoretic union of the triune persons; for example, J.-M. R. Tillard, *Church of Churches: The Ecclesiology of Communion* (Collegeville, MN: Michael Glazier, 1992). For a survey of Catholic approaches to communion ecclesiology, see Dennis M. Doyle, *Communion Ecclesiology: Visions and Versions* (Maryknoll, NY: Orbis, 2000).

2. Avery Dulles, "A Half Century of Ecclesiology," *Theological Studies* 50 (1989): 419–20.

3. Ibid., 422–23. As Dulles notes, according to *Mystici corporis*, no one could be truly a member of the Mystical Body without being a member of the Roman Catholic Church. This teaching caused discontent (if not dissent) among many Catholic theologians.

4. Ibid., 425.

5. Ibid., 427.

6. Ibid., 429.

7. Ibid., 441, and Tillard, *Church of Churches*, xi. This issue continues to be debated among Catholic theologians. See Gerard Mannion, *Ecclesiology and Postmodernity: Questions for the Church in Our Time* (Collegeville, MN: Liturgical, 2007), 52–71.

8. Susan K. Wood, "The Church Is a Communion," in *The Gift of the Church: A Textbook Ecclesiology in Honor of Patrick Granfield, O.S.B.*, ed. Peter Phan (Collegeville, MN: Liturgical, 2000), 163.

9. Susan K. Wood, "Communion Ecclesiology: Source of Hope, Source of Controversy," *Pro Ecclesia* 2 (1993): 425. This paradigm should be not be confused with the "communion" model that Dulles's *Models of the Church* (Garden City, NY: Image Books, 1978) offered as an alternative to the pre–Vatican II preference for an institutional concept, as it emphasizes the intimate fellowship of believers bonded together by "interior graces and gifts of the Holy Spirit" with the "external bonds" only viewed as important "in a subsidiary way" (57). Dulles's first edition was published prior to the 1985 Synod of Bishop's declaration and does not reflect the more developed concept of "communion." Further, Wood and other contemporary Catholic interpreters of Vatican II argue that communion does not replace an institutional understanding of the church but instead grounds it.

10. Susan K. Wood, "Ecclesial *Koinonia* in Ecumenical Dialogues," *One in Christ* 30 (1994): 129.

11. Wood, "Communion Ecclesiology," 426.

12. Wood, "Ecclesial *Koinonia*," 128.

13. Wood, "Communion Ecclesiology," 425.

14. Ibid., 426.

15. Wood, "Church Is a Communion," 162.

16. Ibid., 164.

17. Ibid., 165.

18. See Kilian McDonnell, "The Ratzinger/Kasper Debate: The Universal Church and Local Churches," *Theological Studies* 63 (2002): 227–50.

19. Wood, "Communion Ecclesiology,"425.

20. Wood, "Ecclesial *Koinonia*," 127.

21. Ibid., 131.

22. Ibid., 141.

23. Heinrich Holze, ed., *The Church as Communion: Lutheran Contributions to Ecclesiology*, LWF Documentation 42 (Geneva: Lutheran World Federation, 1997), 13–29.

24. *The Lund Report, The Report as Submitted for the Consideration of the Participating Churches*, Oliver S. Tomkins, ed., The Third World Conference on Faith and Order, Lund, 15–28 August 1952 (London: SCM, 1953), 15–65.

25. Anders Nygren, *Christ and His Church*, The Laidlaw Lectureship, September 1953, trans. Alan Carlsten (Philadelphia: Westminster, 1956), 10. For what follows, see 119–25.

26. For the following, see J. Robert Nelson, *The Realm of Redemption: Studies in the Doctrine of the Nature of the Church in Contemporary Protestant Theology* (Greenwich, CT: Seabury, 1951), 97–104.

27. J. E. Lesslie Newbigin, *The Reunion of the Church: A Defence of the South India Scheme*, rev. ed. (London: SCM, 1960), 60.

28. Ibid., 61.

29. Gustaf Aulén, *Reformation and Catholicity*, trans. Eric H. Wahlstrom (Philadelphia: Muhlenberg, 1961 [1959]), 185.

30. Harold E. Fey, ed., *The Ecumenical Advance: A History of the Ecumenical Movement, Vol. 2, 1948–1968*, 2d ed. (Geneva: WCC, 1970), 151.

31. The term *koinonia* appears in the New Delhi statement of the Third Assembly of the WCC to describe the nature of the church, though without an explicitly trinitarian basis. Third Assembly of the WCC, New Delhi, 1961, "Report of the Section on Unity," in Michael Kinnamon and Brian E. Cope, eds., *The Ecumenical Movement: An Anthology of Key Texts and Voices* (Geneva: WCC, 1997), 89.

32. Brian Flanagan argues that it is Protestants who first used the communion concept to address the division of the church; Catholic interest in the concept initially was focused on the relation between the institutional church and the community undergirding it. See Flanagan, *Communion, Diversity, and Salvation: The Contribution of Jean-Marie Tillard to Systematic Theology*, Ecclesiological Investigations, vol. 12 (New York: T&T Clark, 2011), 24–48.

33. In fact, the World Council of Churches in 1991 introduced the term *communion* as an interpretation and clarification of the term *unity* because the latter was often being interpreted in these negative terms. See Günther Gassman, "The Church is a Communion of Churches," in Carl E. Braaten and Robert W. Jenson, *The Catholicity of the Reformation* (Grand Rapids: Eerdmans, 1996), 94–96.

34. For example, the 1991 World Council of Churches Assembly in Canberra and the official report from the WCC Fifth World Conference on Faith and Order (1993) in Santiago de Compostela both defined the church as *koinonia*. See *On the Way to Fuller Koinonia: Official Report of the Fifth World Conference on Faith and Order*, ed. Thomas F. Best and Günther Gassmann (Geneva: WCC, 1994).

35. Lutheran-Roman Catholic Joint Commission, *Church and Justification: Understanding the Church in Light of the Doctrine of Justification* (Geneva: Lutheran World Federation, 1994).

36. Round X of the U.S. Lutheran-Roman Catholic Dialogue addressed the forms that communion takes in each tradition. See *The Church as Koinonia of Salvation: Its Structures and Ministries*, ed. Randall Lee and Jeffrey Gros (Washington, DC: U.S. Conference of Catholic Bishops, 2005).

37. In 2003, the Tenth Assembly officially added the term *communion* to the LWF name.

38. See Michael Root, "Affirming the Communion: Ecclesiological Reflection in the LWF," in Jens Holger Schjørring, Prasanna Kumari, and Norman A. Hjelm, eds., *From Federation to Communion: The History of the Lutheran World Federation* (Minneapolis: Augsburg Fortress, 1997), 216–46.

39. For the statement itself, see Holze, *The Church as Communion*, 13–29.

40. Ibid., 23.

41. Douwe Visser, "The World Communion of Reformed Churches as a Global Christian Communion," *Reformed World* 60, no. 1 (2010): 5.

42. Ibid., 9.

43. Miroslav Volf offers the most thorough Protestant engagement so far with both Catholic and Orthodox theologians on the communion-ecclesiology paradigm and is commended to the reader for his many insights and trenchant critiques of this paradigm. However, much of his agenda is framed by concerns arising from his free-church background not shared by many mainline Protestants. See Volf, *After Our Likeness: The Church as the Image of the Trinity* (Grand Rapids: Eerdmans, 1998).

44. Robert Jenson, *Systematic Theology*, vol. 1: *The Triune God* (New York: Oxford University Press, 1997), 13. Hereafter, *ST* 1.

45. Robert Jenson, "Proclamation without Metaphysics," *dialog* 1 (1962): 27.

46. Robert Jenson, *Story and Promise: A Brief Theology of the Gospel* (Philadelphia: Fortress Press, 1973), 60.

47. For Jenson, God not only is identified *by* this narrative, but *with* this narrative; *ST* 1:59–60.

48. Ibid., 146.

49. A thorough discuss of Jenson's trinitarian theology is beyond the scope of this book; however, it is worth noting that for Jenson, God's transcendence is understood not as timelessness but radical temporality. Jenson redefines God's eternity as "the unity of Father, Son, and Spirit; the three modes in their temporality are the one God, so that past, present, and future do not fall apart." To avoid collapsing the immanent Trinity into the economic Trinity (and thereby binding God in time), Jenson suggests that we think of the "immanent" Trinity as simply the eschatological reality of the "economic." See Robert Jenson, *God after God: The God of the Past and the Future as Seen in the Work of Karl Barth* (New York: Bobbs-Merrill, 1969), 96, 128.

50. Jenson, *ST* 1:118–19.

51. Jenson, *God after God,* 85, his emphasis.

52. Robert Jenson, *Systematic Theology,* vol. 2, *The Works of God* (New York: Oxford University Press, 1999), 76. Hereafter, *ST* 2.

53. Ibid., 295.

54. Ibid., 297.

55. Ibid., his emphasis.

56. Ibid., 168.

57. Ibid., 173.

58. Ibid., 183.

59. Ibid. 175. Jenson interprets Augustine's concept of the *totus Christus* through Barth's concept of predestination as the election of Jesus Christ together with his people; ibid., 81.

60. Ibid., 178–79.

61. Ibid., 171.

62. Ibid., 173.

63. Ibid., 182.

64. Ibid., 179, 181.

65. Ibid., 193–94.

66. Ibid., 192.

67. Ibid., 196.

68. Ibid., 197.

69. Ibid., 199. Not surprisingly, for Jenson the church's prophecy is the gospel in summary: "Jesus is risen."

70. Ibid., 204. Although Jenson recognizes the important Orthodox critique of Roman Catholic ecclesiology for its pneumatological deficiency, it is not clear to me that his own ecclesiology with its strong emphasis on polity and structure escapes this critique. To be fair,

Jenson does not ignore the role of the Spirit in understanding the church as communion. Except for the Spirit's founding role at Pentecost, however, the only other pneumatological references relating to the church are regarding church order and worship, i.e., charisms for the execution of ecclesial offices and the Spirit's agency (in the *anamenesis*) in the eucharistic celebration. These points seem almost a footnote to the much more robust role given to the Son in Jenson's ecclesiology. See ibid., 179–81.

71. Ibid., 213.

72. Ibid., 214.

73. Ibid., 220. Some fear that Jenson collapses ecclesiology into Christology in a way that *Lumen Gentium* attempted to avoid. See Susan K. Wood, "Robert Jenson's Ecclesiology from a Roman Catholic Perspective," in *Trinity, Time and the Church: A Response to the Theology of Robert W. Jenson,* ed. Colin E. Gunton (Grand Rapids: Eerdmans, 2000), 178, 182. Scott Swain asks, "If the church with her sacraments is truly Christ's body (that is, Christ's availability to the baptized), then "how then can the church also be Christ's bride, his personal other, with whom he is capable of interacting and communing?" Swain, "God According to the Gospel: A Critical Dialogue with Robert W. Jenson on the Hermeneutics of Trinitarian Identification," PhD diss., Trinity Evangelical Divinity School, 2002, 175.

74. *ST* 2:221.

75. Ibid., 223.

76. Ibid., 249 (italics his).

77. Robert Jenson, "How the World Lost Its Story," *First Things* (October 1993): 22–23. Jenson points to the early church as a model: "The ancient church constituted herself a moral world by her liturgy and her churchly discipline," in particular admission to Baptism and Eucharist. Idem, "What Difference Post-Modernity Makes for the Church," *Trinity Seminary Review* 18, no. 2 (1997): 85; and *ST* 2:305.

78. Karel Blei, "Communion and Catholicity: Reformed Perspectives on Ecclesiology," *Reformed World* 55 (2005): 369–79; Daniel L. Migliore, "The Communion of the Triune God: Toward a Trinitarian Ecclesiology in Reformed Perspective," in *Reformed Theology: Identity and Ecumenicity*, ed. Wallace M. Alston Jr. and Michael Welker (Grand Rapids: Eerdmans, 2003), 140–54; and Rubén Rosario Rodríguez, "Calvin and Communion Ecclesiology: An Ecumenical Conversation," *Theology Today* 66 (2009): 154–69.

79. For this section, I draw on Philip Butin's historical work on Calvin's trinitarian theology and Reformed ecclesiology as well as his own systematic work on the Trinity, which has ecclesiological implications and draws explicitly on the language of *koinonia*. While he has yet to write a systematic ecclesiology, there are strong resonances between his work and the communion paradigm. It should be noted that his trinitarian framework also has a strong missional focus. While I am using Butin as a representative of communion ecclesiology, he shares many of the same concerns and impulses that undergird missional ecclesiology.

80. Philip Butin, "Reformed Ecclesiology: Trinitarian Grace According to Calvin," *Studies in Reformed Theology and History* 2, no. 1 (Winter 1994): 1.

81. Philip Butin, *The Trinity* (Louisville: Geneva, 2000), 89.

82. Philip Butin, *Revelation, Redemption, and Response: Calvin's Trinitarian Understanding of the Divine-Human Relationship* (New York: Oxford University Press, 1994), 129.

83. Butin, *Trinity*, 91.

84. Butin, "Reformed Ecclesiology," 3; Migliore, "Communion of the Triune God," 140.

85. Butin, *Revelation*, 130.

86. Ibid., 41, 43. In fact, Butin argues that Calvin will not allow a distinction between the immanent and economic Trinity "because the Word and the Spirit are nothing less than the very essence of God"; ibid., 59.

87. Ibid., 56–60.

88. Ibid., 65.

89. Calvin's doctrine of election was motivated by a twofold ecclesiological concern: to assure believers with certainty of their true membership in the body of Christ and to place the boundaries of the true church beyond human control. Ibid., 99.

90. Butin, *Trinity*, 76.

91. Butin, *Revelation*, 71.

92. Butin, *Revelation*, 77, 83. Calvin went so far as to speak of an inclusion of believers in the perichoresis of the divine life through their participation in Christ by the Holy Spirit.

93. Ibid., 99.

94. Butin, *Trinity*, 97.

95. Ibid., 98.

96. Butin, "Reformed Ecclesiology," 13.

97. Butin, *Revelation*, 120.

98. Ibid., 114.

99. Ibid., 115.

100. Ibid., 119.

101. Ibid., 120.

102. Butin, "Reformed Ecclesiology," 17.

103. Ibid., 34–35.

104. Ibid., 39.

105. Ibid., 41ff.

106. Butin, *Trinity*, 115.

107. Ibid., 93.

108. Nicholas M. Healy, "Ecclesiology and Communion," *Perspectives in Religious Studies* 31 (2004): 274. See also his "Communion Ecclesiology: A Cautionary Note," *Pro Ecclesia* 4 (1995): 442–53.

109. Roman Catholic theologian Bradford Hinze argues that a communion ecclesiology need not develop in a way that threatens inclusivity and diversity, particularly if attention is paid to the pneumatological and dialogical dimensions of ecclesiology; Hinze, review of Dennis Doyle, *Communion Ecclesiology*, *Horizons* 29 (Fall 2002): 331–34.

110. *Communion, Responsibility, and Accountability: Responding as a Lutheran Communion to Neoliberal Globalization*, LWF Documentation 50, ed. Karen Bloomquist (Geneva: Lutheran World Federation, 2004), 269.

111. Neil Ormerod, "The Structure of a Systematic Ecclesiology," *Theological Studies* 63 (2002): 29.

112. See, for example, Holze, *The Church as Communion*, 18. These are, of course, not mutually exclusive. A draft of the working document of the WCC's 1993 statement "Toward *Koinonia* in Faith, Life and Witness" includes "acts of forgiveness and reconciliation" as central to "an authentic life in *koinonia*;" however, the published document omits the reference to "forgiveness," opting for language of renewal and healing of divisions. Cited in Wood, "Communion Ecclesiology," 427.

113. In "Sermon on the Blessed Sacrament of the Holy and True Body and Blood of Christ and the Brotherhoods" (1519), in E. Theodore Bachman, ed., *Luther's Works,* vol. 35 (Philadelphia: Fortress Press, 1960), 45–73. Luther made a connection between communion as "participation in the blessings of Christ" and communion as "participation as a communal activity of mutual sharing among Christians." Luther grounded this not in trinitarian *perichoresis,* but in an idea much like that of the "happy exchange" in "On the Freedom of a Christian" (1520), in Harold J. Grimm, ed., *Luther's Works*, vol. 31 (Philadelphia: Fortress Press, 1957), 333–77.

114. Jenson, "What Difference Post-Modernity Makes for the Church," 88.

115. See Jenson, "How the World Lost Its Story," 22.

116. Butin, *Trinity*, 113.

117. Ibid., 115.

118. Ibid., 116.

4

Ecclesiology Post-Christendom
The Missional Church

While there is much to commend in each of the previous paradigms, both were developed under Christendom and so the questions undergirding them presume a context in which the church's existence and purpose was clear: it was assumed that the faithful would gather. In a post-Christendom context, the church must wrestle with its theological identity and purpose in a society that can no longer assume the centrality and influence of the church in people's lives. Today the question is more basic: *Why the church?*[1] *Why gather in the first place? Why does the church exist at all?* In this chapter, I will discuss a third church concept, the "missional church," which directly addresses this changing context in the United States.

THE GOSPEL AND OUR CULTURE NETWORK
AND THE "MISSIONAL CHURCH"

While many churches are still "dreaming Christendom dreams" and trying to find ways to reclaim their "bring up the numbers," others see the "disestablishment of the churches" as an opportunity for the church to rediscover its identity in this new context.[2] One example is the Gospel and Our Culture Network (hereafter, GOCN) of North America, which formed in the 1990s with a commitment to the missionary encounter of the gospel with North American assumptions, perspectives, and practices.[3] The GOCN self-consciously took up the gauntlet thrown down by Lesslie Newbigin upon returning to his native country of England in the mid-1970s after serving for decades as a missionary and bishop of the Church in South India. Newbigin challenged the churches of the West "to look at our own contexts as missionary settings and to be as rigorous about what that must mean for our own missionary life as we have about mission elsewhere."[4] According to Newbigin, the missionary consciousness of the church has been crippled by several factors. Foremost is the relationship of the church to the state under Christendom (whether actual or *de facto*), which in turn has led to nonmissionary ecclesiological reflection and patterns of church membership as well as the loss of an antithetical tension with culture. The flip side of this is the separation of the church and mission in the modern missionary movement, by which "mission" designates a society for the propagation of the gospel and "church" designates a community that exists to worship and nurture the spiritual lives of its members. Newbigin wrote, "The New Testament knows of only one missionary society—the Church. The eighteenth century knew Churches which had totally ceased to be missionary societies and saw the birth of missionary societies which made no claim to be Churches."[5]

The work of the GOCN over the past two decades has focused in three areas that clearly reflect the influence of Newbigin's work: (1) critical analysis of postmodern North American culture; (2) theological reflection on the gospel to which the church is called to bear witness; and (3) ecclesiological discussion regarding what kind of church is needed to bear witness to the gospel in this new context.[6] Regarding the third area, the GOCN has followed Newbigin in calling for a missionary ecclesiology for the North American context. In order to avoid the historical baggage that comes with the term *missionary*, the adjective *missional* was adopted to emphasize the "essential nature and vocation of the church as God's called and sent people," an understanding of the church that is supported by the New Testament witness.[7] While the term might suggest a functional understanding of the church, it is theologically grounded in the concept of the *missio Dei*. The term *mission* is rooted in classical trinitarian theology and until the sixteenth century was used exclusively with reference to the "missions" of the Son and the Spirit within the Godhead.[8] The *missio Dei* concept adopts this traditional understanding and builds on it, as noted by David Bosch: "The classical doctrine of the *missio Dei* as God the Father sending the Son, and God the Father and the Son sending the Spirit [is] expanded to include yet another 'movement': Father, Son ,and Holy Spirit sending the church into the world."[9] This makes mission "the result of God's initiative, rooted in God's purposes to restore and heal creation. 'Mission' means 'sending' and it is the central biblical theme describing the purpose of God's action in human history."[10] For the GOCN, mission is not something that the church voluntarily does; it is something that God is doing that becomes part of the church's own nature as God calls the church into being and life through the

Spirit. In other words, mission is not primarily an activity or even a purpose of the church; rather, mission is central to the church's identity and nature because the church has been called into being by a "missional" God. "In the emerging ecclesiology, the church is seen as essentially missionary," as Bosch states; "Here the church is not the sender but the one sent."[11] Or as the catchphrase often, perhaps apocryphally, attributed to Rowan Williams famously puts it, "It is not that the church has a mission. God's mission has a church."

Most scholars attribute this shift in the understanding of mission to Karl Barth.[12] Twenty years later, Karl Hartenstein coined the phrase "*missio Dei*" in his report of the Willingen Conference on the International Missionary Council to refer to the purposes and activities of God in and for the whole world, and not just the evangelization of the unreached nations. He wrote, "Mission is not just the conversion of the individual, nor just obedience to the word of the Lord, nor just the obligation to gather the church. It is the taking part in the sending of the Son, the *missio Dei,* with the holistic aim of establishing Christ's rule over all redeemed creation."[13] Along with the universal redemptive focus of God's mission, Willengen stressed the trinitarian foundation of mission: "The missionary movement of which we are part has its source in the triune God Himself. Out of the depths of His love for us, the Father has sent forth His beloved Son to reconcile all things to Himself, that we and all men might, through the Spirit, be made one in Him with the Father, in that perfect love which is the very nature of God."[14] Willingen shifted the central reference point for mission from the church to God, but continued to affirm the christocentric center of God's mission as well as the church as the primary agent of God's mission in the world.[15]

This understanding of *missio Dei* was challenged in the 1960s, leading to an alternative vision of mission for which the Dutch missiologist J. C. Hoekendijk was perhaps most responsible.[16] For Hoekendijk, the world is the arena of God's mission and the focus is placed on the ways that God works outside of the church to create shalom in society. This shalom is "at once peace, integrity, community, harmony, and justice." Further, "This concept in all its comprehensive richness should be our leitmotif in Christian work. God intends the redemption of the whole of creation."[17] This makes the church's role somewhat superfluous, relegated to giving testimony to how God is working in the world to bring about shalom. Lutheran missiologist James Scherer offers this critique: "For Hoekendijk, it appeared, *missio Dei* had become identified with a process of historical transformation whereby humankind would gradually achieve the goals of the messianic kingdom through the processes of secular history."[18] However, Hoekendijk's world-centered concept of mission greatly influenced the work of the World Council of Churches and Konrad Raiser, the former secretary general of the WCC, who entered into a public debate with Newbigin over the question of the *missio Dei* and the role of the church in it.

These two "forms" of *missio Dei* represented by Newbigin and Raiser are known respectively as the classical (or special) form, and the ecumenical (or general) form. The ecumenical form follows Hoekendijk's critique of the classical form, which is that the classical form is too christocentric and too focused on the church and salvation history. Raiser also wants to replace universal salvation history with the *oikumene*, the world, as the central image for God's mission, and in particular, solidarity among all life forms as the goal of God's mission. The church shares in God's mission by joining what God is doing already in the world through the Spirit. As Michael Goheen states, "Fearing the Christomonistic and triumphalist tendencies of Christocentrism, Raiser wants to stress a trinitarianism that gives full scope to the working of the Spirit."[19]

While appreciating these concerns, Newbigin wonders how one can adopt a trinitarian framework that is not centered in the life, death, and resurrection of Jesus Christ. For Newbigin, a trinitarian perspective "can only be an enlargement and development of a Christo-centric one and not an alternative set over against it, for the doctrine of the Trinity is the theological articulation of what it means to say that Jesus is the unique Word of God incarnate in world history."[20] By not giving the church a distinct role in God's mission, the universal significance of Jesus Christ is eclipsed and the distinction between the church and the world is collapsed. For Newbigin and others who hold a "classical" view of *missio Dei*, the church is a distinctive community called by God to be an instrument, sign, and first fruit of God's inbreaking kingdom.[21]

Newbigin's work was foundational to the agenda of the GOCN, central to which is to develop a missionary ecclesiology for the changing American context, which has become a new kind of mission field.[22] In 1998, six leaders within the GOCN movement coauthored *Missional Church: A Vision for the Sending of the Church in North America*. This has become a key text for the movement and reflects the influence of Newbigin's work, especially with regard to his critique of Christendom. The main argument of the book can be summarized by six "movements:"[23] (1) the church in North America is now located within a dramatically changed context; (2) the good news of the gospel announced by Jesus as the reign of God needs to shape the identity of the missional church; (3) the missional church with its identity rooted in the reign of God must live as an alternative community in the world; (4) the missional church needs to understand that the Holy Spirit cultivates communities that represent the reign of God; (5) the missional church is to be led by missional leadership that focuses on equipping all of God's people for mission; and (6) the missional church needs to develop missional structures for shaping its life and ministry as well as practice missional connectedness within the larger church. Since its publication, there seems to be no end to the number of books being published addressing the "missional church."

In spite of its seminal nature, a number of underdeveloped concepts and unresolved theological issues remain. These have been addressed by Craig Van Gelder, a contributing author to *Missional Church*, and Dwight Zscheile. Two issues especially are pertinent to this discussion. First, while the *missio Dei* concept is used in the book, no reference is made to the history of its development and the competing visions that have emerged. Thus it is unclear how the authors intend the concept to be understood. A more developed discussion not only could have clarified this, but also explored an integrated approach of the two visions, one that could affirm a more expansive view of God's reign without forsaking a specific role for the church.[24]

The second issue relates to the trinitarian foundation of a missional ecclesiology. Two approaches to understanding the work of God in the world in trinitarian terms can be found in the text. The first understands the work of God primarily through the life, death, and resurrection of Jesus Christ, positing an ecclesiology "shaped primarily by the message of Jesus and responsible for embodying and emulating the life that Jesus lived."[25] The other takes the work of the Spirit as the entry point, proposing an understanding of the church "shaped primarily by the power and presence of the Spirit, who creates, gifts, empowers, and leads the church into engaging in a series of ecclesial practices."[26] While the authors no doubt intended these approaches to be complementary, Van Gelder and Zscheile believe that they did not adequately integrate the sending work of God in relation to the work of the Son and the work of the Spirit.[27] They attribute this to a reliance on a Western view of the Trinity that lends itself to modalistic[28] tendencies and defines God as a "sending God," in contrast to an Eastern view and its understanding of the Trinity in communal, perichoretic terms.[29] A fresh view of missional church could be developed were one to take "communion" as a complementary principle to "sending" for understanding the nature of the Trinity and the *missio Dei.* These two approaches, christological and pneumatological, are reflected in the missional ecclesiologies that have emerged from two GOCN authors, respectively Darrell Guder and Craig Van Gelder.

DARRELL GUDER'S INCARNATIONAL WITNESS

Darrell Guder is a key figure in the GOCN, serving as editor and contributing author for *Missional Church* and authoring a second book in the GOCN series.[30] His first monograph already addresses issues that would become central to the work of the GOCN.[31] Guder believes that the church has been influenced and co-opted by Western, Enlightenment ideas, especially by defining mission in terms of progress, success, the benefits of Western culture, and "expansionism." As heirs of the Christendom legacy, the church has inherited a reductionism of salvation (whereby salvation is understood in terms of where one spends eternity rather than in terms of the inbreaking kingdom of God) and of the church (whereby the church is viewed as the dispenser of this "salvation" rather than a witness to the kingdom of God). Along with other GOCN authors, he points out the weaknesses of classical Reformation ecclesiology for the task of mission in our context today. Specifically, he criticizes the Reformers' view of the church only as a means of grace and not as a witnessing community. The church needs to reclaim its identity in terms of the church's unique calling, that is, to be a witness to the kingdom of God. Guder agrees that the church first must face the ways it has been captive to the wider culture before it can reclaim this identity and vocation. The church does this through its own conversion.[32] Conversion is necessary, Guder argues, because of the ways the church has sought to control the gospel over the centuries of Christian history; for example, in the historical tendency of the Western church to forge an uneasy marriage between gospel and "the benefits of Western civilization"[33] or in attempts to submit the gospel to a political agenda. The "continuing conversion" of the church happens as "the Christian community discovers that the claims of Christ and his gospel confront its sinfulness, reveal the drive to control the gospel and uncover its compromises with its environment."[34] As the church is itself evangelized through "continuing conversion," it in turn is enabled to evangelize others.

While he contends that one problem with evangelization[35] is that it has not been rooted in a trinitarian framework of the *missio Dei*, his own theology of evangelization is strongly christocentric. Guder focuses on the entire event of Christ's life, teaching, proclamation, passion, and resurrection; however, it is in the resurrection that the message and the messenger, the king and the kingdom come together. For this reason, he states, the church's ministry of evangelization must be understood and practiced as the "form" or "actualization" of the kingdom of God.[36] His key concept for this ministry is "witness," which "provides a common missiological thread through all the New Testament language that expounds the church's mission" and "serves as an overarching term drawing together proclamation (*kerygma*), community (*koinonia*), and service (*diakonia*). These are all essential dimensions of the Spirit-enabled witness for which the Christian community is called and sent."[37] Guder recognizes the primary place of proclamation in the Reformation traditions, but he cautions that this emphasis has led to a narrow understanding of witness, whereby it has become relegated to oral communication by pastors to laypeople in the gathered worshiping community. He is critical of those who would restrict the kergymatic reality of the word to the preaching event, as some followers of Karl Barth do.[38] For him, witness incorporates far more than the speaking and hearing of the gospel message. "It is the demonstration in the life and activity of God's people of the tangible fact that God's rule is breaking in among the disciples of Jesus Christ."[39]

Guder goes on to develop these ideas ecclesiologically. The church is an essential part of the gospel because the church is the "agency" by which God's saving acts in Christ might be known to the world. He draws together the image of the church as the body of Christ with the notion of the church as witnessing community drawn from Acts into what he calls an "incarnational" understanding of the church's nature and mission.[40] Keenly aware of the problems associated with a pre–Vatican II concept of the church as a prolongation or extension of the incarnation,[41] he instead adopts—though still with caution—the adjective *incarnational*. By it he means that the unique event of the incarnation of Jesus Christ that constitutes and defines the message and mission of the church has particular significance not only for the understanding, but also the practice, of Christian witness.[42] This has several implications. First, witness must be embodied by a community, and not only by individuals. In particular, "the witness to Jesus Christ is incarnated in the formation of the church as the missional community; Jesus Christ forms his church for its incarnational witness by making disciples who become apostles."[43] Second, witness includes not only sharing the gospel in words, but also in action and being.[44] Finally, the content of the church's witness is also incarnational. Because the church is "actualizing" the kingdom of God, its witness is holistic. It cannot be reduced to one aspect of the good news (such as the forgiveness of sins) but is inclusive of reconciliation, healing, redemption, and hope. As Guder states, "It is not possible to describe the healing and saving purposes of God too comprehensively. Incarnational witness is fundamentally open to the continuing discovery of surprising ways in which God heals what we have long come to regard as broken."[45]

Ultimately, the mission of the church is to embody in its communal life God's love in Christ for the world. For Guder, this is the heart of the matter, and the reason that Jesus called the church into being. As in all aspects of discipleship, this must be learned from Jesus himself, who gave his church the commandment to love another as he has loved them. Guder recognizes that churches will not live out this incarnational witness perfectly; indeed, the church is often quite unloving in its communal life and witness. This is why, according to Guder, "the community incarnates its witness to love in no other way more profoundly than in its honest admission of its own sin and its continuing growth toward the fullness of that love. In other words, the community enfleshes the gospel of love as it lives out its forgiveness before all the world."[46]

Craig Van Gelder's Spirit-Created and Spirit-Led Community

Craig Van Gelder, also a Reformed theologian, is another key figure in the missional church movement. He proposes a *missio Dei* concept of the church that begins with the activity of the Holy Spirit, which also continues to shape the activity of the church—a community created and led by the Spirit. He contrasts the missional church model with those of the established church (the European state church model) and what he calls corporate church (which includes aspects of the voluntary association model). He is likewise critical of two common approaches to the crisis in which the church finds itself in light of the changing context of North America: the functional approach, which defines the church in terms of what the church does, and the organizational approach, which defines the church in terms of its structure and organization. For Van Gelder, the solution to the crisis facing the church today lies not in doing something new or restructuring the church, but in rediscovering the church's nature or being. For him the critical question is "What is the church?" His answer, which draws on the insights of the *missio Dei* concept, is "a community created by the Spirit."[47] He writes, "The continuing erosion of the functional 'Christendom' developed within the U.S. and Canada, each with its own type of churched culture, is forcing new discussion of what it means to be the church in North America. . . . now that the church no longer has a privileged position within North American culture, it is rediscovering its fundamental missionary identity to live as a new community demonstrating God's redemptive reign in the broader society."[48]

Van Gelder discusses the significance of the shift from the creedal marks of the church (one, holy, catholic, and apostolic) to the two Protestant "marks" of word and sacrament for ecclesiology. While appreciating the intent of the

Reformers to reestablish the church's primary calling to proclaim the gospel, he notes that attention to these marks led later Protestants to focus more inwardly than outwardly, as ways to distinguish the true church from the false—as well as the basis on which to separate from the false church. In his view, an ecclesiology founded on word and sacrament can lead to a reductive view of the church and questions related to structures of authorization of ministers for the indispensable ministry of word and sacrament.[49] He is equally critical of the free-church movement as a resource for a missional ecclesiology, since its focus was primarily on the organization of the church rather than its theological basis. He asserts that the idea of the "free church" became embedded in the U.S. context and coalesced with the voluntary principle, leading to the development of the "corporate church," a church defined by function more than by nature or being, and its corollary structure of the national denomination.[50]

Instead, like Guder, he turns to the New Testament and the concept of the redemptive reign or kingdom of God. Rather than something the church is called to "build, establish, or promote," the New Testament teaches that the relationship of God's people to God's reign is rather one of "seeking, entering, receiving, and inheriting."[51] As Van Gelder states, "The church is a people shaped by the redemptive reign of God. The church is not an end in itself. It has a distinct calling—to demonstrate the reality of God's redemptive power in the world. It has a unique nature—to live as a fellowship that demonstrates kingdom values and expresses kingdom power. It has a distinct purpose of carrying out a ministry of participating fully in the redemptive work of God in the world."[52] He understands God's redemptive work in terms of creation, re-creation, and consummation. His narration of salvation history begins with Genesis and draws on covenantal language, reflecting his Reformed background.

The nature of the church, then, is defined by the mission of God in the world and as the result of Christ's redemptive work. Van Gelder defines the church as a community "created by the Spirit, the result of the Spirit's implementation of God's reign in human history."[53] He points to four core biblical images for the church that develop the theme of the church as a social community which is both human and divine, local and universal, and one and diverse: (1) the people of God, (2) the body of Christ, (3) the communion of the saints, and (4) the creation of the Holy Spirit.[54] While he offers brief reflections on *koinonia* in his discussion of the third image, he does not engage the vast literature on ecumenical ecclesiology and its central paradigm of communion/*koinonia*. He emphasizes the apostolic nature of the church in his discussion of the Nicene "marks" of the church, emphasizing the "sending" aspect of apostolicity.[55]

The church is led and taught by the Spirit in the living out of its ministry, which he defines in covenantal terms as reconciliation.[56] His follow-up book, *The Ministry of the Missional Church: A Community Led by the Spirit* (2007), fleshes out these ideas in more detail. He brings together theology and organization theory to offer a practical theology for congregations seeking to become missional communities. He reviews the ministry of the Holy Spirit in both Old and New Testaments in the redemptive reign of God and focuses on the leading aspect of the Spirit's ministry for congregational ministry in the face of changing contexts. For Van Gelder, because the missional church is a Spirit-led church, an awareness of the Spirit's role is central to understanding the participation of the church in God's mission to the world.[57]

An Assessment of the Missional-Church Ecclesiology

Both Guder and Van Gelder clearly begin with the post-Christendom context; both understand the church as sent as well as gathered and both note the limitations of classic Reformation ecclesiology for the challenges facing the churches today. Both ground their ecclesiologies in the reign of God that breaks in through the life, death, and resurrection of Jesus Christ. Both stress the communal aspect of mission: the church is a community whose nature is determined by the inbreaking kingdom of God and God's call to the church to participate in this kingdom. Their differences lie in the way they arrive at this point. Guder calls for the church to be "incarnational," stressing the narrative of Jesus' own life, at times seeming to call for an imitation. Van Gelder, on the other hand, gives the Spirit a central role in his ecclesiology, calling for a Spirit-created and Spirit-led church.

Both also point to the reality of the church as a community and stress that the church's life in community constitutes its witness to the world. While proclamation holds a central place, it does not exhaustively define the church's purpose and mission, as can be the case in some word ecclesiologies. By New Testament definition, the witness of the church is broader, encompassing also *koinonia* and service. I find especially compelling Guder's vision for how the church embodies this new life, albeit imperfectly; that is, as a community who lives out the gift of reconciliation and forgiveness before the world, as a people who are *simul iustus et peccator*.[58]

The main difficulty I have with Guder's proposal is that without a developed pneumatology, Guder has no means by which to articulate how the incarnational witness of the church happens, except through submission to and imitation of Christ, which can suggest a voluntary aspect to his church concept. While he appeals to a trinitarian *missio Dei* framework and acknowledges the role of the Holy Spirit in mission, such references are minimal[59] and stress a more instrumental (for example, he refers to the Holy Spirit as "empowerment") than personal understanding of the Holy Spirit. He writes that as the church learns to embody Christ's love, it can be an instrument of the Holy Spirit, and "to the degree that the community resists the practice of that radical love it is less useful to the work of the Holy Spirit."[60] Guder fears that grounding ecclesiology in the Third rather than the Second Article of the Apostles' Creed would mean a shift to religious experience or spirituality and a downplaying of the uniqueness of Christ.[61] As I will show, this need not be the case when one works within a trinitarian and narrative framework whereby the church's "story" *continues* into the creed's Third Article. Further, the theological category that the creed uses to describe this embodiment is not incarnation but sanctification or "making holy."

Van Gelder's attention to the role of the Spirit in his ecclesiology therefore is most welcome. While I appreciate his designation of the church as a community that is "Spirit-created" and "Spirit-led," I wish he had wrestled more theologically with the person and work of the Holy Spirit who creates and leads the church. His designation of the church as a "community led by the Spirit" does not capture the fullness of the Spirit's role in the life of the church. In an otherwise appreciative review of *The Ministry of the Missional Church*, Les Longden notes that Van Gelder's use of "Spirit-led" seems superficial and unsubstantiated. "We read constant references to the leading of the Spirit but are given no description of what this 'leading' might look like."[62]

Van Gelder proposes a fuller trinitarian foundation for a missional ecclesiology that draws on the resources of Eastern theology, especially the idea of the Trinity as a perichoretic communion of persons to complement the idea of the Trinity as a "sending" God. While he seems unaware of the rich literature of *koinonia* ecclesiology that has emerged in the West in recent years (as well as the East), he is correct to suggest that a missional ecclesiology would be enriched by engaging the concept of "communion." That is one of the purposes of this book: to bring the strengths of all three of these ecclesiological paradigms—word, communion, *missio Dei*—into conversation with each other.

The word-event paradigm retains the Reformation focus on the proclamation of the forgiveness of sins as a gift that comes to us from outside of ourselves (*extra nos*), as a word that is addressed to us and creates the community of the church. The communion paradigm emphasizes that this gift is not only declared but is the gift of Christ himself present in faith to believers that enables them to share communion with the Triune God through incorporation into the body of Christ, centrally through participation in the Eucharist. Through this incorporation, we are also enabled to share in a *koinonia* of love with other members of the body of Christ and reflect God's desire for communion with all creation. The primary limitation of the word-event and communion paradigms is that they do not take into account the post-Christendom context in the same way as the missional paradigm. The *missio Dei* paradigm puts the focus on God's action both in creating and gathering the church through word and sacrament, as well as sending it, which is why I have chosen it as my starting point from which to address the question "Who is the church?" in our post-Christendom context today.

Further, while both the communion and *missio Dei* paradigms offer a trinitarian foundation for ecclesiology, I am giving preference to the *missio Dei* paradigm because, as Neil Ormerod points out, the attempt to ground ecclesiology in the Trinity by means of *communio* and *perichoresis* poses difficulties because "the divine unity is where God is most different from God's creatures, even the creation that we call church. What is first in our knowledge of the triune nature are the divine missions of Word and Spirit, which in turn ground our knowledge of the processions and persons of the Trinity."[63]

Stephen Bevans has proposed that we think of the Holy Spirit as "God inside out." With Rahner's famous "rule" in mind (that is, "The immanent Trinity is the economic Trinity, and the economic Trinity is the immanent Trinity"), he proposes that "*God's* 'inside,' i.e. God's mystery, can only be known from God's 'outside,' i.e. God's movement to creation in Mission. Furthermore . . . this movement is accomplished in the first place through the action of the Holy Spirit. God's deepest nature, in other words, is discerned not by focusing on God's inner Trinitarian, communal life, but on God's 'ec-centric,' 'centrifugal' reaching out to the world in love."[64] Bevans rightly identifies the activity of the Holy Spirit as the first way that God reaches out to the world. "The Spirit is divine mystery sent from "inside" to be that mystery fully present and active "outside"—in the world, in human history, in human experience: the Spirit is God Inside Out."[65] The church is created by and as a part of this movement of the Spirit outward. It is in this *missio Dei* that the church finds it identity and purpose. As we have seen, the classical doctrine of *missio Dei* is defined as God the Father sending the Son, and God the Father and the Son sending the Spirit, a movement expanded to include Father, Son, and

Holy Spirit sending the church into the world. But the reverse of this actually reflects the order of God's activity in the world. That is, the *missio Dei* begins with the Spirit.

For Reflection and Discussion

1. How is the trinitarian basis of the missional-church paradigm similar to, and different from, the communion paradigm? What are the central elements of this paradigm?

2. Historically, what are the two forms of the *missio Dei* concept? Which one has more promise for a twenty-first century ecclesiology? Why?

3. How does the missional-church concept acknowledge and respond to the post-Christendom context as compared to the previous two paradigms?

4. How do Darrell Guder and Craig Van Gelder develop their respective ecclesiologies using the theological starting point of the *missio Dei*? What similarities and differences do you see in these authors, especially with regard to the identity and purpose/mission of the church?

5. What are the contributions of the missional-church paradigm to the ecclesiological discussion today? How does starting with the "mission of the Triune God" help you think differently about the identity and purpose of the church in today's context? What elements of this paradigm should be retained for a contemporary ecclesiology for post-Christendom age? How would your congregation respond to the ideas in this paradigm?

6. What are the weaknesses of this paradigm? How might this paradigm be strengthened by theological engagement with the communion paradigm? The word-event paradigm?

Notes

1. The phrase is from *Why the Church?*, ed. Walter J. Burghardt and William Thompson (New York: Paulist, 1977).

2. Darrell L. Guder, ed., *Missional Church: A Vision for the Sending of the Church in North America*, The Gospel and Our Culture (Grand Rapids: Eerdmans, 1998), 70, 77.

3. The GOCN has been holding annual consultations since the early 1990s and has published in partnership with Wm. B. Eerdmans several titles in "The Gospel and Our Culture" series. For a full listing, see http://www.gocn.org/.

4. George Hunsberger, "The Newbigin Gauntlet: Developing a Domestic Missiology for North America," in George Hunsberger and Craig Van Gelder, eds., *The Church Between Gospel and Culture: The Emerging Mission in North America*, The Gospel and Our Culture (Grand Rapids: Eerdmans, 1996), 3–25. The following is drawn from Michael W. Goheen, "'As the Father has sent me, I am sending you': Lesslie Newbigin's Missionary Ecclesiology," *International Review of Mission* 91, no. 62 (2002): 354–69.

5. Lesslie Newbigin, *The Reunion of the Church: A Defence of the South India Scheme* (London, SCM, 1948), 10.

6. Michael W. Goheen, "The Missional Church: Ecclesiological Discussion in the Gospel and Our Culture Network in North America," *Missiology: An International Review* 30, no. 4 (2002): 479–90.

7. Guder, ed., *Missional Church*, 11. The term is not a neologism. See also Craig Van Gelder and Dwight J. Zscheile, *The Missional Church in Perspective: Mapping Trends and Shaping the Conversation* (Grand Rapids: Baker Academic, 2011), 42–46. A former student of mine, Matthew Kruse, prefers to make "missional" a genitive in English, like it would be in Greek; thus being a missional church is a church "belonging to mission."

8. David J. Bosch, *Transforming Mission: Paradigm Shifts in Theology of Mission*, American Society of Missiology Series, no. 16 (Maryknoll, NY: Orbis, 1991), 1.

9. Ibid., 390.

10. Guder, ed., *Missional Church*, 4.

11. See Bosch, *Transforming Mission,* 372.

12. Ibid., 389–93; see also Van Gelder and Zscheile, *Missional Church in Perspective*, 15–40.

13. Cited by Tormod Engelsviken, "*Missio Dei*: The Understanding and Misunderstanding of a Theological Concept in European Churches and Missiology," *International Review of Mission*, 92, no. 367 (October 2003): 482n6.

14. Ibid., 482.

15. Ibid., 486.

16. Ibid., 487.

17. Johannes Christiaan Hoekendijk, *The Church Inside Out,* ed. L. A. Hoedemaker and Pieter Tijmes, trans. Isaac C. Rottenberg (Philadelphia: Westminster, 1966), 19–20.

18. Engelsviken, "*Missio Dei*," 489.

19. Michael W. Goheen, "The Future of Mission in the World Council of Churches: The Dialogue between Lesslie Newbigin and Konrad Raiser, *Mission Studies* 21, no. 1 (2004): 99; Bosch, *Transforming Mission*, 391.

20. Lesslie Newbigin, "Ecumenical Amnesia," *International Bulletin of Missionary Research* 18 (1994): 2.

21. Goheen, "Future of Mission," 104–105.

22. Craig Van Gelder, "A Great New Fact of Our Day: America as a Mission Field," in Hunsberger and Van Gelder, eds., *Church Between Gospel and Culture,* 57–68.

23. These are taken directly from Van Gelder and Zscheile, *Missional Church in Perspective*, 49–52.

24. Ibid., ch. 4, "Expanding and Enriching the Theological Frameworks."

25. Ibid., 53.

26. Ibid., 54.

27. Ibid.

28. The heresy of modalism, which arose in the third century, overemphasizes the unity of the Trinity at the expense of the distinctness of the three persons whereby the Father, Son, and Holy Spirit are understood as being three modes or manifestations of one divine Person.

29. It is beyond the scope of this work to address this claim, but this is an oversimplified view of the differences between Eastern and Western trinitarian theology. As seen in the previous chapter, Western theologians have been robustly engaging communion theology in this same vein for the past fifty years or longer.

30. Guder, ed., *Missional Church*; and idem, *The Continuing Conversion of the Church*, Gospel and Our Culture (Grand Rapids: Eerdmans, 2000).

31. Darrell L. Guder, *Be My Witnesses: The Church's Mission, Message, and Messengers* (Grand Rapids: Eerdmans, 1985).

32. Guder, *Continuing Conversion*, 26–27.

33. Ibid., 91.

34. Ibid., 97–98.

35. Guder's preferred term to "evangelism"; see Guder, *Be My Witnesses*, 136.

36. Guder, *Continuing Conversion*, 44–46.

37. Ibid., 53.

38. Ibid., 61; and idem, *Be My Witnesses*, 49.

39. Ibid., 62.

40. Guder, *Be My Witnesses*, 28–32.

41. Ibid., 18–19.

42. Guder, *The Incarnation and the Church's Witness*, Christian Mission and Modern Culture (Harrisburg, PA: Trinity Press International, 1999), xii–xiii, 15.

43. Ibid., 21.

44. Guder, *Be My Witnesses*, 91.

45. Guder, *The Incarnation*, 33.

46. Ibid., 46.

47. Craig Van Gelder, *The Essence of the Church: A Community Created by the Spirit* (Grand Rapids: Baker Books, 2000), 24.

48. Ibid., 43.

49. Van Gelder, *Essence*, 56–57, 143.

50. Ibid., 67. I disagree with Van Gelder's assertion that the free-church movement had a major impact on "American ecclesiology," at least in the mainline traditions, as few are "free church" in their theology or polity.

51. Ibid., 87.

52. Ibid., 89.

53. Ibid., 126.

54. Ibid., 107.

55. Ibid., 123.

56. Ibid., 139, 142.

57. Craig Van Gelder, *The Ministry of the Missional Church: A Community Led by the Spirit* (Grand Rapids: Baker Books, 2007), 118.

58. Guder, *Incarnation*, 23.

59. They are also more prevalent in his earlier book, *Be My Witnesses*, than in his later works.

60. Ibid., 40, 59.

61. Ibid., 13.

62. Les Longden, review of *The Ministry of the Missional Church*, in *Journal of Religious Leadership* 9, no. 1 (2010): 125.

63. Neil Ormerod, "The Structure of a Systematic Ecclesiology," *Theological Studies* 63 (2002): 29.

64. See Stephen Bevans, "God Inside Out: Notes toward a Missionary Theology of the Spirit," *International Bulletin of Missionary Research* 22 (1998): 102.

65. Ibid.

5

Starting with the Spirit
A Narrative Method for Ecclesiology Post-Christendom

In this post-Christendom context, the central question being asked of the church is not only a question of purpose or function; it is fundamentally one of identity: "Who is the church?" To answer this question theologically suggests beginning with the identity and purpose of God. Rather than begin with God's address to us in the word or God's own being as a communion of persons, I have suggested starting with the *ad extra* movement of God in the *missio Dei*. In this chapter, I propose that narrative is the method most proper to exploring the church's identity in light of this movement of God and that this narrative should be read pneumatologically, that is, from the perspective of what God the Holy Spirit is doing.

I propose using a narrative method to answer the question of the church's identity that explores both the "story of the church" in the Holy Scriptures and, as I will suggest in the following chapter, by extension to the Third Article of the Apostles' Creed, in answering the question of church's identity. As Edmund Schlink has pointed out, the church exists in a double—not a single—movement of the Spirit. Following the New Testament narrative, the church is both the people of God called *out* of the world and *sent into* the world.[1] In between these movements, the Spirit-breathed church finds its identity as a "communion of saints" who live by the gift of "the forgiveness of sins," and in the Spirit-enabled living out of this gift, becomes and is a witness to the world. A narrative method that "starts with the Spirit," then, offers a way to think about the identity of the church that incorporates the missional focus of the third paradigm but also the theological contributions of the other two paradigms: the emphasis on the word in proclamation encountering hearers from outside of themselves to bring reconciliation with God through the forgiveness of sins, and the communion that members share with God and one another as a gift of God's own self-giving.

A Narrative Method

In theological study, a narrative method is, broadly speaking, one that draws upon literary theories employed in the modern analysis of narrative literature. Such a method derives insights from literary criticism and applies these insights to theological reflection. Even though narrative method in theology has been associated primarily with George Lindbeck and others in the "Yale School," according to L. Gregory Jones, "There is not so much a distinct position known as 'narrative theology' as there are a variety of ways in which theologians have argued for the significance of narrative for theological reflection."[2] A primary reason for employing a narrative method is that it solves the problem of using "identity" as a category. To speak of the church's "identity" rather than its nature or being might suggest to some the sociological method used in "identity studies" wherein a group's identity is determined over and against the identity of other groups.[3] This can contribute to an "us-and-them" mentality that can create obstacles for mission. While the church does have a peculiar and distinctive identity, this is found not in its identity over and against "others" but, rather, in relationship to the One who is "Other," God, whom we know through the revelation given to us in Scripture.

There are two other reasons for using a narrative method for exploring the identity and purpose of the church. Narrative resonates with the sensibilities of the postmodern, post-Christendom context, which are drawn to understand reality relationally, through story and narrative, rather than through propositionally stated, universal truth-claims. This leads to my second and perhaps most important reason: a narrative approach to ecclesiology is especially appropriate for the church in the United States today because, as I showed in chapter 1, the history of the U.S. Protestant mainline churches have been shaped by a particular narrative, one that subsumed the scriptural story of the church toward a new *telos*—that of a "Christian America."[4] Amidst the breakdown of the narrative of a Christian America, the church is offered a new opportunity to rediscover its missional identity in the story of the Scriptures. As Charles Van Engen states, "The view of Scripture as a tapestry of God's action takes seriously both the vertical multiplicity of historical contexts and cultures in which biblical revelation occurs, and the horizontal continuity of God's disclosure in history, with particular emphasis on God's mission (*missio Dei*)."[5] A narrative method explores the identity of the church by considering its place in the story of Scripture in terms of its relationships, character, and purpose.

In spite of the fact that narrative promises to be a worthwhile method for ecclesiology, few theologians have explored the natural connection between narrative, ecclesiology, and mission, especially for the American context.[6] Neither has narrative been used explicitly as a method in the three ecclesial paradigms considered in the previous chapters, although Robert Jenson appeals to narrative in his larger theological project. Even though he grounds his theology, especially the doctrine of the Trinity, in the narrative of Scripture, he does not follow this same method in developing his doctrine of the church. He does appeal to the scriptural narrative in his initial discussion of the *founding* of the church, but shifts gears when he comes to the *nature* of the church and adopts an Augustinian ontology, which leads him to emphasize the church's structure and offices. Nonetheless, the argument can be made that, underlying Jenson's ontological description of the church's nature, there *is* a kind of narrative structure. However, this narrative does not begin with the coming of the Holy Spirit at Pentecost or even the election of Israel, but with the delay of the Spirit to usher in the parousia, making the church an eschatological "detour."[7] "The story of the church" emerges for Jenson in scriptural texts like the pastoral epistles, which emphasize the order and peace of the church and suggest a structure by which the church's unity can be guaranteed during this in-between time.[8] In effect, Jenson answers the question "Who is the church?" not with a narration of the church's story, but with a description of the church's order and structure.

We saw in chapter 4 that although Darrell Guder does not explicitly invoke a narrative method, he points to the story of Jesus as the pattern for the church's life and mission. In a different way, Natalie K. Watson proposes an incarnational narrative method for feminist ecclesiology.[9] She describes the life of the church as being both bounded and open: bounded by the story of Jesus Christ, "the story which is embodied and told by those who share in it," and open to all people and all of God's creation. Watson does not engage the biblical text in any specifics, however, in making her proposal. Instead, she emphasizes the continuing story of the church, told not only by those past saints who offered their lives in witness to God (in both the scriptural narrative or later tradition), but also by women struggling to reclaim the authority that the patriarchal church has denied them for so long. Indeed, for Watson, church happens in the sharing of stories: "That women, men and children begin to find spaces in which they can flourish and live in relationships of justice, is rooted in the story of the Triune God sharing God's own being with humankind and in doing so sharing their being." The "larger story" in which these are told is the story of the incarnation. The story of our humanity is rooted in the story of God's sharing the struggle and pain of humanity in the incarnation.[10]

One of the more ambitious attempts at a narrative ecclesiology is that of ecumenist and Lutheran theologian George Lindbeck,[11] who allegedly has been working on this project for nearly twenty years. Unlike Guder and Watson, he does not begin with the life of Jesus but with the story of Israel.[12] Because of Lindbeck's significant contributions to narrative theology and because of the centrality of Israel to the church's own story and identity, it seems appropriate to consider his approach in some detail before offering my own proposal.

George Lindbeck's Israel-Like Ecclesiology

Lindbeck's theological method can be described as a classical and canonical narrative reading of the whole Scripture, combined with historical-critical awareness[13] and shaped by his own cultural-linguistic theory of religion, wherein religion operates like a language whose grammar must be learned, or a culture whose habits must be inculcated. James Massa notes that while Lindbeck offers his cultural-linguistic theory to better understand inter-Christian differences, at the same time he has been "laying the groundwork for an ecclesiology that looks to healing the primordial 'division' of Christianity, namely, that between the church and synagogue."[14]

Lindbeck's "ecumenically mandated" vision of the church, then, is the "the messianic pilgrim people of God typologically shaped by Israel's story."[15] Although sympathetic to supersessionist concerns,[16] he prefers the "people of God" concept as the doctrinally and ecumenically warranted starting point for thinking about the church.[17] He notes its centrality in the Second Vatican Council's Constitution on the Church. Because it is also congenial to evangelical concerns, it has an ecumenical advantage over other concepts like sacrament and body of Christ. Most important is that the church claimed Israel's story as its story. As he states, "They were that part of the people of God who lived in the time between the times after the messianic era had begun but before the final coming of the kingdom. Whatever is true of Israel is true of the Church except where the differences are explicit."[18]

Lindbeck offers four heuristic guidelines for reading the New Testament references to ecclesiology. First is the recognition that the story of the people of God is logically prior to any images of the church or list of marks of the church. In a narrative ecclesiology, the story determines the concepts rather than being determined by them. A corollary of this is the recognition that the "church" refers first and foremost to concrete groups of people who exist in time and space, who have a history. As he notes, "An invisible Church is as biblically odd as an invisible Israel."[19] Third, Israel's history is the church's history and their Bible is the Hebrew Scriptures. To be sure, it is read through the Christ event, but it is the church's only communal "story."[20] The final guideline is to recognize that, for the early Christians, Israel and the church are one people. The church does not replace Israel as the new "people of God," as in the secessionist view; rather, "the people of God" enlarges to include Gentile believers in Christ. A new epoch—not a new people—is formed with the resurrection of Jesus and the outpouring of the Holy Spirit on all flesh. With this new epoch come "unheard-of possibilities and actualities" of new life, but not a new identity.[21]

Because "Christendom is passing and Christians are becoming a *diaspora*,"[22] the situation is ripe for a return to "Israel's story as a template which helps shape Christian community." Like Israel, the church needs to reclaim its identity as the people of God chosen or elected to testify to God's glory. This means that the identity of the church is grounded first and foremost on God's irresistible call, and this election is recognized by specific marks, such as Baptism. The church consists of all who have been elected by God, whether or not they are responding to the mark of their election. Further, this election is communal. It is a people who are chosen; individuals are only chosen as a result of their inclusion into the elect community.

Second, the primary mission of this elect people is not to save souls, but to witness faithfully to the God who alone judges and saves. As Lindbeck puts it, "It testifies to this God whether or not it wills to do so, whether or not it is faithful or unfaithful."[23] The church's witness is its communal life as the elect people of God, the body of Christ. In this way, the church serves as "the communal sign of the promised redemption, in the time between the times."[24] The church accomplishes this primarily by tending to its own internal life, by building up its own body, and not by responding to the needs of humanity everywhere. Through the mutual building-up of its body, the church becomes a liberating force in the larger world and a light to the nations.[25]

Lindbeck points to three practices that shape both the church's communal identity and mission: (1) worship and doxology, (2) communal repentance, and (3) obedience to God's commandments. Lindbeck stresses the role of worship as central in the church's mission in the world. He writes, "The fundamental witness of the elect peoples to the coming Kingdom is in being communities which whole-heartedly laud and bless the Holy Name."[26] If the church is to be a "light to the nations," however, the church first must repent of the divisions within its own community, that is, the disunity of Christians with each other and with Jews. The pattern for this communal repentance is the story of Israel. Lindbeck writes, "Only by gazing at itself in the mirror of Israel can the church as a whole learn how to lament biblically for its intramural and extramural divisiveness and lovelessness."[27] This requires individuals to remain within the church and exercise their prophetic vocation, which is to call others to remain loyal to the community and to warn it against further disintegration.[28]

Like Israel, the life of the church (which is its witness) is also built up through obedience to God's commandments. He appeals to the "the pastoral and catechetical Luther," who, like the rabbis, regarded the Decalogue as the "preeminent text" in terms of a practical guide to shape the "total form of whole communities in every sphere of life, economic, political and familial and religious,"[29] providing "an all-embracing order for human existence."[30] In this sense, obedience is a response to the narrative of Scripture that proclaims the history of God's gracious dealings with humankind in creation, in the coming of the Messiah, and in the gathering of the church by the Holy Spirit.[31] As these stories are appropriated by faith *pro me* (to use a favorite phrase of Luther's), Lindbeck proposes, "they become one's own story, they elicit the fear, love and trust of God above all things, which, according to Luther, is the sum and substance of the first commandment and without which we cannot rightly obey any of the others."[32] Obedience may be understood as a narrative response to justification; those to whom God gives the gift of faith will accept his Lordship and obey him. The justified community finds its identity in its obedience to the rules or grammar given to shape its life together.[33]

For Lindbeck, then, the church finds its communal identity and mission in the story of Israel. The story of Israel is the type for the church's story. The church (as part of an expanded Israel) is the people of God whose identity and mission (like Israel's) are shaped by its obedience to God's commands (in response to God's gracious acts), its communal repentance, and its doxological worship. As he states, "The ecclesiology of the apostolic writing is, one might say Israel-ology. Everything that their Scripture, viz. the Old Testament, says about Israel can apply also to the Church except what is implicitly or explicitly excluded. Thus, the ecclesiological silences of the New Testament, which are many, can be rightly filled with Old Testament material."[34]

While I agree that it is important to stress the continuity between Judaism and Christianity, I will argue below that there are differences in the church's own story that point to a particular role or calling that is not shared in the same way by the rest of Israel. Lindbeck does not consider the pneumatologically driven narrative understanding of the identity and mission of the early church in the New Testament (especially the Acts of the Apostles); more surprising is the absence of any discussion of the role that the Holy Spirit plays in the larger biblical narrative.[35]

This narrative also identifies elements distinctive to the church's missional understanding that are not shared by Israel. In particular, I would point to (1) the church's witness to Jesus, sharing the good news of the resurrection through proclamation, wonders, and signs; and (2) the centrality of forgiveness of sins to that proclamation and the life of the new community, in communion with Christ and one another, as dual aspects of the church's early witness.[36] Lindbeck's emphasis on the church's own communal repentance—as important as that prophetic word is for the church today—ignores the very particular directive given to the disciples by their Lord "that repentance and forgiveness of sins is to be proclaimed in his name to all nations, beginning from Jerusalem" (Luke 24:47). As David Bosch points out, although God's compassion embraces all nations and not just Israel, "Israel would, however, not actually go out to the nations. Neither would Israel expressly call the nations to faith in Yahweh."[37] As a people within "expanded Israel," the church does have a particular witness that is not shared by Israel as a whole, central to which is the proclamation of the resurrection of Jesus Christ and the gift of forgiveness of sins that is available "in his name." Rather than define the church's mission by its practices, as Lindbeck's cultural-linguistic method seems to warrant, the narrative of the New Testament defines the church by the movement of the Holy Spirit in its proclamation. This movement not only enables these practices but also a new life in Jesus' name, lived out in *koinonia*, at the heart of which is the gift of forgiveness of sins and the breaking down of personal, cultural, and social barriers.

A NARRATIVE ECCLESIOLOGY THAT "STARTS WITH THE SPIRIT:" THE ACTS OF THE APOSTLES

My goal in this section is to explore more fully a narrative ecclesiology that "starts with the Spirit." The first question to answer is: Where in the biblical narrative should one start? Although the church's own story is rooted in the story of Israel and the ministry of Jesus, I contend that the church receives its *particular identity and purpose* through the Holy Spirit, which in the Acts narrative is promised by Jesus after his resurrection and received at Pentecost. As Gerhard Krodel notes, it is not until the outpouring of the Holy Spirit in

Luke-Acts that the disciples become "what they have not yet been, witnesses of Jesus and of his resurrection."[38]

The thorny question of the relationship between the church and Judaism cannot be engaged in detail here, but I propose a mediating position between Lindbeck's position (the church is Israel) and the more traditional view that the church succeeds Israel as God's people.[39] At Pentecost, the Holy Spirit gives the church a distinctive identity and calling within Israel as *a part* of God's people.[40] The church is called to witness to Jesus (Acts 1:8)[41] and to offer forgiveness of sins in his name, thereby becoming a certain kind of community, a *koinonia,* as part of this witness.[42] Although the Spirit was active among God's people long before being promised and poured out at the Pentecost event recorded in Acts—for instance, Israel's judges and the prophets—the Spirit's indwelling is experienced in a more universal and permanent way at Pentecost and as the Spirit of Christ, the Holy Spirit, possesses a personal character and quality "which before it could not have been clearly perceived."[43] In Acts, we see these two themes—*the people of God* called to be *witnesses to Jesus*—come together in a distinctive way to give the church its particular Spirit-breathed identity and purpose. While the phrase "Spirit-breathed" has been used to describe a view of the Holy Scriptures (based on 2 Timothy 3:16), a narrative reading of the Scriptures suggests that it is a more appropriate description for the church. Thus, in both John and Luke-Acts, the Spirit is breathed or blown on the disciples, giving them a new identity and mission to forgive sins (John 20:22-23) and to be witnesses to Jesus' resurrection (Acts 1:8).

The story of this Spirit-breathed people is told in the Acts of the Apostles, the only "story of the early church" we have in the New Testament.[44] Historically, Acts has largely been neglected by mainline Protestants as a resource for ecclesiology, and not only because of questions regarding its historical accuracy. In the previous century, Luke had been viewed as "the first representative of evolving early Catholicism, *früh Katholizismus,* and Luke's "Gentile theology" has been variously conceived as bearing the seeds of ecclesiastical hierarchy and episcopacy and as replacing the *theologia crucis* of Paul with a *theologia gloriae.*[45] Acts also has been associated with the church-growth movement, which can lead to a different kind of theology of glory that focuses on the numerical growth of the church as evidence of God's blessing.[46] While I do not want to minimize such concerns, these reflect rather narrow readings of the Acts narrative.[47]

Although recent scholarship on Acts has stressed the importance of literary and narrative criticism, only very recently has the role of the Holy Spirit been considered specifically in narrative terms. Most biblical scholarship on the role of the Holy Spirit in Acts in the past few decades has focused on a debate over whether its role is soteriological or missiological.[48] According to William H. Shepherd, this debate has failed to consider the narrative role of the Holy Spirit in Acts, instead asking questions of Luke that he never set out to answer and using tools (historical-critical) that are largely foreign to his chosen genre (Luke 1:1).[49] Shepherd's narrative approach leads him to propose that the Holy Spirit in Acts is "God's on-stage representative" who offers literary reliability of God's promises. As Luke's audience is primarily Gentile, with few Jewish Christians remaining, they are left to question God's reliability regarding the apparent "failure" of God's promises to God's chosen people. The purpose of Luke-Acts, then, is to show that God did first fulfill God's promises to Israel before extending them to the Gentiles. It is the narrative role of the Holy Spirit to ensure the reliability of God's promises by guaranteeing the prophetic word.[50] While Shepherd helpfully points to narrative criticism as the appropriate method given Luke's genre, his own thesis does not really consider the Holy Spirit as a character in its own right, but as more of a literary device. Or as Ju Hur states, Shepherd is describing the narrative effect of the Holy Spirit on the reader more than the narrative role of the Holy Spirit in the plot of Acts, the latter which Shepherd fails to consider in any detail.[51] Hur's own narrative proposal considers the Holy Spirit not only in terms of its character but its function in the overall plot of Luke-Acts. He concurs with the majority view of biblical scholars that for Luke, the Spirit primarily has a charismatic-prophetic function, meaning that the Holy Spirit reveals God's will and purpose through human agents, charismatic leaders like judges, kings, and prophets.[52] The "plot" of Luke-Acts, according to Hur, is "the way of witness, in seeking and saving God's people engendered by Jesus (in the gospel) and his witnesses (in Acts) through the power and guidance of the Holy Spirit in accord with the plan of God."[53] Following the line of thought in the previous chapter, we may describe the plot of Acts in terms of the *missio Dei*, in a missional movement directed by the Spirit to include all people in God's promise of salvation.[54]

Hur identifies three roles for the Holy Spirit in relation to the church in the Acts narrative. First is the Spirit as mission director, guiding and directing the church's witness by giving prophetic speech to various leaders in the church, who are described as being "filled with the Spirit" in order to witness to Jesus. The heart of this witness is the promise of salvation and the forgiveness of sins through the resurrection. The Holy Spirit not only gives the disciples boldness for their witness (4:29, 31) but also sometimes speaks at decisive moments in the narrative when specific guidance is needed, especially with regard to the mission to the Gentiles.[55] A second and related role assigned to the Holy Spirit is as the "verifying cause" by which certain groups are incorporated into God's eschatological people. The Holy Spirit not only directs the mission but the outcome of the mission, breaking down age-old barriers and prejudices. A third role is to supervise and sustain those in Christian community or *koinonia*. In what follows, I consider these three roles more fully with regard to the church's Spirit-breathed identity and purpose.

THE IDENTITY AND PURPOSE OF THE SPIRIT-BREATHED CHURCH IN ACTS

At the end of Luke's Gospel, Jesus tells his disciples that they are "witnesses" of his death and resurrection and "that repentance and forgiveness and sins is to be proclaimed in his name to all nations, beginning from Jerusalem" (Luke 24:47). He then says that he is sending upon them "what my Father has promised," and tells them to stay there until they are "clothed with power from on high." Both of these phrases, "promise of the Father" and "power from on high," reappear at the beginning of Acts (1:4, 8) as references to the Holy Spirit with whom they will be baptized (Acts 1:5). A number of scholars interpret this "power from on high" or "baptism in the Holy Spirit" as an additional empowerment for the ministry of witnessing, connecting the Holy Spirit to mission but not to salvation.[56] As Mark Allan Powell points out, Luke does not explicitly refer to the Holy Spirit as bringing people to faith or salvation, nor does he make an explicit connection between the Spirit and the moral life. Indeed, it seems that Luke "ignores or neglects these aspects of the Holy Spirit's work in order to concentrate on the one function he considers indispensable: providing Jesus' disciples with power to be witnesses (1:8)."[57] As noted above, it is commonly held that Luke's pneumatology is fashioned after the Old Testament understanding of the Spirit of prophecy, in contrast to Paul's more soteriological pneumatology or to Johannine pneumatology, which stresses the life-giving function of the Spirit. These themes are not absent in Luke-Acts, however, especially considered in relationship to the restoration of Israel, which many scholars now recognize plays a significant role in Luke's theology.[58]

The Old Testament prophets attributed the restoration of Israel to the working of the Spirit (Isa. 32:15, 44:3, 59:21; Ezek. 36:27, 37; 39:29; Hag. 2:5; Zech. 4:6, 6:8, 2:10).[59] During the exilic and postexilic periods, the coming restoration and renewal were articulated primarily in terms of a transformation and renewal of the people by the Spirit. The Spirit is understood as a divine force that brings life in every aspect of the restored nation. Like Joel, Isaiah uses the language of the Spirit being "poured out" to effect this transformation in Isaiah 32:14 and 44:3. As Wonsuk Ma notes, the creation language of Isaiah 44:3 "reinforces the life-giving effect of the Spirit, which results in growth both numerically and spiritually."[60] Elsewhere, the prophets describe the change explicitly in terms of a new heart and new spirit (Ezek. 36:26-27).

In the Pentecost event described in Acts 2:1-11, the Holy Spirit appears like a violent and loud wind (*pneuma*) that filled the house, and as tongues like fire that rested on each believer. The resulting gift of communication in which believers both speak and hear in different languages is often cited as fulfillment of the Joel text that Peter cites in his sermon (Acts 2:14-36, esp. 2:17). The Holy Spirit endows those gathered with the ability to speak prophetically in a way that enables communication and brings about unity. Against the backdrop of this broader prophetic tradition, however, the outpouring of the Holy Spirit must also be seen as an eschatological event that cleanses hearts and brings new life. In the Old Testament, according to Hans Walter Wolff, "the pouring out of God's Spirit upon flesh means the establishment of a new, vigorous life through God's undeserved giving of himself to those, who, in themselves, are rootless and feeble, especially in the approaching times of judgment."[61] The people called to new life shall be a nation of prophets, and the purpose of "the new prophetic relationship to God is manifest in an authorized calling upon the God who calls."[62] The prophetic language of "pouring" is reiterated in 2:33 ("having received from the Father the promise of the Holy Spirit, [Jesus] has poured out this that you both see and hear"), a promise that is "for you, and for your children, and for all who are far away, everyone to whom the Lord our God calls to him" (2:39). For Luke, the promise includes not only the reception of the Holy Spirit, but also renewal and new life through the forgiveness of sins in Jesus' name (Acts 2:28-39; 5:31-32; 10:43).[63] Later in Acts, we see the same connection made between the Holy Spirit and "repentance that leads to life" (11:18) and cleansing of hearts by faith (15:7-9).

As the Holy Spirit restores and cleanses the disciples in this eschatological outpouring, the Spirit also empowers them to share the word boldly—even and especially in the face of persecution (4:31). While Luke draws on the Old Testament understanding of the Spirit of prophecy, he goes beyond this tradition by linking the Spirit with the capacity to witness concerning the suffering, death, and resurrection of Jesus and the preaching of the forgiveness of sins.[64] We see Peter embody this capacity in his proclamation given in the midst of "prophesying" that occurs when the Spirit is outpoured (Acts 2:14-36), where, as we saw, he explicitly connects the gift of the Holy Spirit with the forgiveness of sins. Later in Acts 5:31-32, Peter interprets the events of Jesus' death and exaltation as the means by which God "might give repentance to Israel and the forgiveness of sins." He goes on to say, "We are witnesses to these things," along with the Holy Spirit (named here in personal terms as a witness alongside of the disciples). The disciples are to witness to "these things," that is, the death of Jesus Christ and the gift of forgiveness in Jesus' name (Luke 24:47; Acts 13:38).[65] Their "mission field" is to be all nations, beginning in Jerusalem. In the book of Acts, the Spirit is the agent in the narrative who is "breathed" upon those gathered in order to grant forgiveness of sins, and to enable the proclamation of that gift to others (Acts 2:43).

The Spirit has a third role in the Acts narrative, which is to draw those who have been renewed by the Holy Spirit deeply into communion with God and each other. We read in Acts 2:42 that the new believers "devoted themselves to the apostles' teaching and fellowship [koinonia], to the breaking of bread and the prayers." Paul specifically describes koinonia as a gift of the Spirit (2 Cor. 13:14), but as John Reumann points out, it is less a synonym for church in the New Testament (except by way of 1 Corinthians 10:16) than it is a description of its character or way of being in the world. It refers "to that which believers are called, namely fellowship with Christ and the Spirit, participating in the blessings of Jesus' death and being a part of Christ's body, through faith, with responsibilities for mission, care of the saints locally and in Jerusalem, and hospitality and benevolence."[66] Luke's portrayal of the community in Acts 2:44-47 echoes this way of life, as they are described in terms of togetherness and generosity, in which they share all things in common with a specific concern for the needy among them and for the goodwill of all people (2:44-47). In his second description of ecclesial community in Acts 4:32-37, Luke does not repeat the use of the word koinonia, but the believers are said to be of "one heart and soul" and the description of their shared common life strongly echoes the description in Acts 2:42-47.

In the Acts narrative, we not only see the Spirit present to create fellowship and growth (2:47), but also to convict members who do not put koinonia first and who let their sin and greed get the best of them, as illustrated by the story of Ananias and Sapphira (Acts 5:1-11). The immediate context for this story is the description of community life in 4:32-35 noted above. With this as the background, to "lie to" or "tempt" the Spirit means to resist the restoring power of the Spirit, which is creating among the people of Israel a new kind of community. As Luke T. Johnson notes,

> The community was constituted as 'one mind and heart' by the Spirit of God. It was the Spirit that led them to call nothing their own and share all their possessions. But this couple 'falsified the Spirit' in the first place by their breaking the unanimity of intention; they 'colluded' in their action. They were hoping that by counterfeiting the gesture, they could both partake of the community life and 'hold back something of their own'. . . . The couple's biggest mistake was thinking that they were dealing with simply another human gathering.[67]

The Spirit, who is described in very personal terms here (as someone who can be lied to and tested), not only creates *koinonia*, but also convicts believers who are not living according to it.

It seems pertinent here to note that one of Luke's preferred terms for the church is "the Way" (Acts 9:2; 18:25-26; 19:9, 23; 24:14, 22). This has been interpreted by some as a "pilgrim people on the move,"[68] but in light of the above, I think a better understanding is in terms of "way of life" or "way of being." To be people of "the Way" means to be shaped by the Spirit to live a certain way, the way of new life in Jesus' name. The Scripture references above support this view, as believers are said to "belong to the Way" (9:2) and be "instructed in the Way" (18:25); there is an appropriate way to worship, "according to the Way" (24:14). The community that emerges from and is shaped by the outpouring or breathing of the Spirit, is called and enabled by the Spirit to belong to "the Way," living by repentance and forgiveness, and in a *koinonia* of sharing with God and one another. The church is oriented both toward this promise of a renewed life and toward "the other," those with whom the promise is to be shared.[69]

The book of Acts narrates the expansion of this *koinonia* geographically, numerically, and ethnically. The Holy Spirit is the primary missionary in this movement, or as Hur puts it, "the mission director." Although the disciples receive a charge from Jesus in Luke 24:47 and Acts 1:8, they are not "sent out" in the same way as in Matthew 28:18-20 or John 20:21. In Luke-Acts, "the only sending mentioned is that of the promised Spirit."[70] The Son sends the Holy Spirit to direct the disciples in their witness (whether willing or not) that will expand the people to God to include all nations. The Spirit drives the apostles out of their comfort zones and across ethnic and other boundaries to witness to the power of the resurrection to bring forgiveness and new life to *all* people. As the mission director, the Holy Spirit speaks to, directs, makes decisions for and with the apostles (e.g., 13:2, 4; 16:6-7), and as we already have seen, is a witness alongside of them (5:32).

Three subsequent "fallings" of the Spirit serve as major narrative turning points in this expansion: on the Samaritans in Acts 8; on the Gentiles in Acts 10-11, which is later referred to in Acts 15; and finally on the Ephesian "disciples" in Acts 19.[71] Although these three episodes have been at the center of the "baptism of the Spirit" debate,[72] Luke's point in relaying them is not to lay out a "theology of reception" but to indicate the *missio Dei*, that is, the mission of God to expand the eschatological people of God by the movement of the Spirit across seemingly impenetrable boundaries. In Ju Hur's words, the Spirit acts as "verifying cause" by which these groups are included into the *laos* (people) of God, by falling on them in the same way the Spirit fell on those gathered at Pentecost.

In Acts 8:14-17, Luke tells of the reception of the Holy Spirit by the Samaritans. The most obvious narrative purpose in mentioning the Samaritans is that Samaria is one of the geographical signposts mentioned in Jesus' mission "charge" to the Twelve just before his ascension (1:8). In this episode, the Samaritans are included in God's eschatological people, and on one level is another instance of the Spirit reaching out to the marginal and outcast.[73] But the Samaritans have a larger, symbolic role in Israel's history. This "turning point" in the narrative actually allows for the next step, the inclusion of Gentiles. They are not Gentiles, as a comparison of Acts 8 with Acts 10–11 shows,[74] but at best they are "the lost sheep of Israel."[75] As David Ravens notes, "The Samaritans are a stepping stone to the Gentile mission because there is a theological imperative to show signs of the healing of the old division of Israel."[76] He continues: "Without the return of the Samaritans there could be no restored Israel and without Israel in the process of restoration there would be nothing for the Gentiles to enter."[77] If we look at this episode as a template of the Spirit's work in the church today, we need to consider what "close relationships" within (and between) our denominations need to be healed by the Spirit in order to strengthen the church's witness to the world. This episode suggests that part of the Spirit's missional work is to heal divisions within the family of faith: in the case of the Acts narrative, the "old division" between Israel and Samaria, and in the case of the church today, old and new divisions between and within denominations, including "family fights" over issues such as sexuality and biblical interpretation. As I suggest in the next chapter, an aspect of the church's witness is how its members live with and treat one another. The old and new divisions, if we resist the Spirit's work to heal them and insist on holding onto old grudges and hurts, will remain obstacles to church's witness to those outside of its walls, those who do not yet believe.

This episode is followed by the story of the Ethiopian eunuch's conversion and baptism by Philip, which is worth noting as it includes two references to the Spirit explicitly directing the missional movement of the church. An angel directs Philip to Gaza along the wilderness road, but then it is the Spirit who speaks directly to Philip, telling him to go to the chariot, where a court official of Candace, queen of the Ethiopians, is reading from the prophet Isaiah (Acts 8:28-29). The Ethiopian eunuch is an "other" in two ways: ethnically and sexually. Ethnically, he is not a Jew but a foreigner; and even if he is a proselyte, he can never fully become a Jew because as a eunuch he cannot participate in the life of the Temple (Lev. 21:20; Deut. 23:1). This episode offers a glimpse of the wider boundaries that the Spirit will cross in service to the *missio Dei*, in order to bring all people into God's promise.

The next—and most significant—"turning point" is Luke's narration of the conversion of the house of Cornelius in Acts 10–11, and its interpretation by Peter and James at the Council of Jerusalem in Acts 15.[78] Luke's intention here is clear: the outpouring of the Spirit on the Gentiles is to be understood as a sign of their inclusion into God's eschatological people: "And I remembered the word of the Lord, how he said, 'John baptized with water, but you shall be baptized with the Holy Spirit. If then God gave the same gift to them as he gave to us when we believed in the Lord Jesus Christ, who was I that I could withstand God?" (11:17).

Indeed, the Holy Spirit is a witness of God's election of the Gentiles, as Peter reiterates later at the council: "And God who knows the heart bore witness to them, giving them the Holy Spirit just as he did to us; and he made no distinction between us and them, but cleansed their hearts by faith" (15:8). Unlike the other two "outpouring" episodes, the Holy Spirit does not come upon the Gentiles indirectly, through the laying on of hands by the apostles. Here the Spirit acts directly, interrupting Peter's sermon, in order to "witness" itself to those present that God no longer makes a distinction between peoples. This is not the only point in the narrative that the Spirit acts directly, of course. The Spirit speaks to Peter, giving him explicit directions twice (10:19; 11:14), as part of the "the lengths God went to overcome the reluctance of Jewish Christians to preach the word to Gentiles."[79] This suggests that part of the Spirit's role is to direct even those who are unwilling to participate in God's mission.

The Gentile reception of the Holy Spirit "amazed" the Judaizers in the crowd because "the gift of the Holy Spirit had been poured out even on the

Gentiles" (10:45). They are amazed because until now, the Spirit belonged only to Israel, and as such, was a sign of God's election and restoration. With the conversion of Cornelius and his household, however, there is no disputing that the Gentiles have also now received "repentance unto life" (11:18). The immediate result of their reception of the Spirit is to speak in tongues and extol God, in an "authorized calling upon the God who calls."

At the Council of Jerusalem, where the decision was made to allow Gentiles to become part of God's people without first becoming Jews, the Holy Spirit is referred to again in personal terms as one who directed the decision for how Jewish and Gentile Christians now ought to live together: "It seemed good to the Holy Spirit and to us to impose on you no further burdens than these essentials" (15:28). As a template for the church's mission today, the Gentile episode teaches us that the Spirit's mission is one of radical inclusion of the "the other," especially those racially and ethnically "other." If we consider it missionally, it challenges the parochial nature of many congregations, not to mention denominations, in terms of ethnic identity.

The third and final "falling" episode occurs in 19:1-7, upon a group of "disciples" at Ephesus who had "never heard of the Holy Spirit." In most cases "disciples" would normally refer to Christians; only as the narrative proceeds does the reader learn that it must refer to the disciples of John the Baptist. Luke tells the reader that these "disciples" have been baptized into John's baptism (19:3).[80] One wonders why Luke would include this episode, especially after the incorporation of the Gentiles into the people of God. Shepherd suggests that it gives literary closure to one of Luke's major subplots: "John the Baptist, one of the main figures of Luke's Gospel, looked forward to the coming of Messiah Jesus, and now the disciples taught by him have come into the community established by Jesus and his disciples through the Spirit."[81] That may be, but we might ponder what this group might signify for the narrative of the church today. If the previous "fallings" had to do with those who were religiously or ethnically "other" than the Jews, these disciples were "other" in that they were still waiting for the promise of salvation to come to them. Today we might call these people "seekers," those who desire to know God but, as Reggie McNeal and Diana Butler Bass remind us, often show up at church and find God "conspicuously absent."[82]

CONCLUSION

In the New Testament, the church receives its distinctive character from the new life of the resurrection given by the Spirit. The Spirit that Jesus breathes onto his disciples is the same Spirit that raised him from the dead (Rom. 8:11), creating a people who live in *koinonia* and walk in the "Way" of the resurrection and the gift of forgiveness, being led and empowered by the same Spirit who indwells them. In contrast to the fearfulness driving much conversation about the church today, we see in Acts glimpses of a community that is oriented toward the possibility of a new communal life and that does not fear its own future survival. Although Luke does not use the language of *missio Dei*, he presents a picture of mission very much in line with it. We see the same Spirit who was breathed on the disciples directing them outside of their comfort zones, pushing them to cross religious, ethnic, and social boundaries, creating *koinonia*, and proclaiming salvation to all. The narrative in Acts sketches out an identity and purpose not only for the church of the first century, but for the church today.

For Reflection and Discussion

1. Do you agree with the author that narrative is a helpful method for discovering the identity of the church? Why or why not?

2. There are a number of possible "starting points" for a narrative ecclesiology. If you were to "tell the story of the church," where might you begin?

3. Do you agree with George Lindbeck that "the church is Israel"? What are the strengths and weaknesses with this narrative approach for a twenty-first-century ecclesiology?

4. How does a narrative ecclesiology that "starts with the Spirit" incorporate elements of the three previous paradigms?

5. How does the Holy Spirit as a "character" in the narrative of the Acts of the Apostles give the church its identity and direct its mission? How would our thinking about the crisis of the church shift if we were to consider the Holy Spirit's narrative role in a similar way today? In other words, how does the narrative in Acts sketch out an identity and purpose not only for the church of the first century, but for the church today?

6. The author suggests that the three later "fallings" of the Spirit on the Samaritans, the Gentiles, and the disciples of John the Baptist can serve as templates of the Spirit's work in the church today. Specifically, these episodes invite us to ponder: (a) What "close relationships" within (and between) our denominations need to be healed by the Spirit in order to strengthen the church's witness to the world today? (b) How does the Spirit's role in Acts challenge the

parochial nature (especially in terms of ethnic identity) of many congregations? (c) How might we be more aware of—and be better witnesses to—those "seekers" around us, many of whom are already be prompted by the Spirit to know God more fully?

Notes

1. Edmund Schlink, *Ökumenische Dogmatik: Grundzüge* (Göttingen: Vandenhoeck & Ruprecht, 1983), 566, my trans.

2. L. Gregory Jones, "Narrative Theology," in *The Blackwell Encyclopedia of Modern Thought*, ed. Alister E. McGrath (Oxford: Blackwell, 1993), 395–98.

3. I thank Jon Pahl for raising this concern.

4. Allen R. Hilton agrees the appropriate method for exploring the church's identity in the U.S. context today is narrative, arguing that all communities take on a story-formed character. Hilton, "Who Are We? Being Christian in an Age of Americanism," in *Anxious about Empire,* ed. Wes Avram (Grand Rapids: Brazos, 2004), 150.

5. Charles Van Engen, *Mission on the Way: Issues in Mission Theology* (Grand Rapids: Baker Books, 1996), 45.

6. A welcome exception is Michael W. Goheen, *A Light to the Nations: The Missional Church and the Biblical Story* (Grand Rapids: Baker Academic, 2011).

7. I thank Gary Simpson for this insight. See Robert Jenson, *Systematic Theology*, vol. 2: *The Works of God* (New York: Oxford University Press, 1999), 204–10.

8. Ibid.

9. Watson agrees that "the question cannot merely be: *What* is the church?, but *Who* is the church?" Natalie K. Watson, *Introduction to Feminist Ecclesiology*, Introductions in Feminist Theology, ed. Mary Grey, Lisa Isherwood, and Janet Wooten (Cleveland: Pilgrim, 2002), 9. Part of the pain has been the ways that women have been excluded both from the story of the church and the telling of it. See Watson, "Reconsidering Ecclesiology," *Theology and Sexuality* 14 (2001): 73.

10. Watson, *Introduction*, 118.

11. Lindbeck's involvement in the ecumenical movement is longstanding. From 1962 to 1964, he served as one of sixty or so Delegated Observers at the Second Vatican Council. He also served as a participant in the first eight dialogues (1965–1990) of the Consultation between the U.S.A. National Committee of the Lutheran World Federation and the Catholic Bishops' Commission for Ecumenical Affairs.

12. See George Lindbeck, "Confession and Community: An Israel-like View of the Church," and, idem, "The Church," in *The Church in a Postliberal Age,* ed. James J. Buckley (Grand Rapids: Eerdmans, 2002), 1–9, 145–65; and "The Story-Shaped Church: Critical Exegesis and Theological Interpretation," in *Scriptural Authority and Narrative Interpretation*, ed. Garrett Green (Philadelphia: Fortress Press, 1987), 161–78.

13. Lindbeck, *Church in a Postliberal Age*, 234–36.

14. James Massa, "Lindbeck's Vision of the Church," *The Thomist* 67 (2003): 466.

15. Lindbeck, *Church in a Postliberal Age,* 146.

16. Lindbeck argues that the historical-critical method has helped unmask supersessionism as an early Christian error that "resulted from self-serving gentile Christian misappropriation of intra-Jewish polemics over Jesus' messiahship. . . . But if these errors are rejected, so I have come to think, Christians can now apply Israel's story to themselves without supersessionism or triumphalism." Ibid., 8.

17. Ibid., 148–49.

18. Ibid., 149.

19. Ibid.

20. In terms of text, Lindbeck is correct; however, he does not take into account the oral Jesus tradition that became foundation for the apostolic kerygma which gave shape to the New Testament.

21. Ibid., 151.

22. Ibid., 153. Lindbeck is more ambiguous about the passing of Christendom than is Douglas John Hall. "The waning of cultural Christianity might be good for the churches, but what about society? To my chagrin, I find myself thinking that traditionally Christian lands when stripped of their historic faith are worse than others. They become unworkable or demonic." Ibid., 7.

23. Ibid., 157.

24. Ibid., 159.

25. Lindbeck recognizes that this focus will seem "outrageous to some in view of the world's needs, but it can be a strength for those who see the weakening communal commitments and loyalties as modernity's fundamental disease." Ibid., 9. This does not mean sectarianism, because the church's communal self-interest necessarily intersects with service to others. For its own sake, the church must seek and pray for the welfare of the earthly cities in which Christians live. Ibid., 251–52.

26. Ibid., 249–50.

27. George Lindbeck, "The Church as Israel: Ecclesiology and Ecumenism," in *Jews and Christians: People of God*, ed. Carl E. Braaten and Robert W. Jenson (Grand Rapids: Eerdmans, 2003), 94.

28. Ibid. Lindbeck does not acknowledge the full breath of the prophet's role in the Old Testament narrative. The prophets not only call Israel to national repentance and unity, they also promise restoration and renewal (e.g., Ezekiel 36–37), gifts made possible by the Spirit. There is no reference to pneumatology in Lindbeck's discussion of prophecy, neither in his narration of Israel's history, nor in the event of Pentecost.

29. Lindbeck, *The Church in a Postliberal Age*, 36.

30. Ibid., 31.

31. Ibid., 25–26.

32. Ibid., 25.

33. Lindbeck finds in the narrative of Israel the foundation for an ecumenically catholic understanding of church structures, including the episcopacy and papacy. The story of Israel shows both the necessity of changing leadership structures to fit new circumstances and needs as well as the importance of continuity and tradition and the authorization of these structures by God. Ibid., 160–65.

34. Ibid., 238.

35. Lindbeck's lack of attention to pneumatology is all the more surprising in light of his desire to stress the narrative continuity between the Old and New Testaments.

36. See Luke 1:77 for forgiveness as a promise given to Israel in the new age.

37. David J. Bosch, *Transforming Mission: Paradigm Shifts in Theology of Mission*, American Society of Missiology Series 16 (Maryknoll, NY: Orbis, 1991), 19. "So if there is 'missionary' in the Old Testament, it is God himself who will, as his eschatological deed par excellence, bring the nations to Jerusalem to worship him there together with his covenant people."

38. Gerhard Krodel, "The Holy Spirit, the Holy Catholic Church: Interpretation of Acts 2:1-42," *dialog* 23 (1984): 97.

39. For a spectrum of views, see Joseph B. Tyson, ed., *Luke-Acts and the Jewish People: Eight Critical Perspectives* (Minneapolis: Augsburg, 1988).

40. Jacob Jervell points to the characteristic role of the Spirit in identifying the church as part of God's people. This is seen most clearly in the reception of the Holy Spirit by the Gentiles,

acknowledged by Luke as proof that they are now part of the people of God. Jacob Jervell, *The Theology of the Acts of the Apostles* (Cambridge: Cambridge University Press, 1996), 42–43.

41. There is some debate among scholars whether Jesus' charge in Act 1:8 applies only to the twelve, or by extension, to all later disciples of Jesus. For example, see Peter G. Bolt, "Mission and Witness," in *Witness to the Gospel: The Theology of Acts*, ed. Howard I. Marshall and David Peterson (Grand Rapids: Eerdmans, 1998), 191–214. I agree with the latter position, as witnessing to Jesus is certainly an aspect of discipleship all Christians share on account of their baptism. If, as I suggest, we may take the missional narrative of Acts as a template for the church's identity and purpose today, then it is appropriate to apply this role to all members of the church.

42. Tertullian wrote in the third century that the pagans were amazed by this, stating: "See how they love one another." Tertullian, *Apology* 39:7.

43. Alexander R. Vidler, *Christian Belief* (London: SCM, 1950), 1–62, cited in Mark Allen Powell, *What Are They Saying about Acts?* (New York: Paulist, 1991), 51.

44. Biblical scholarship has increasingly appreciated the narrative conventions of Acts as "a story." The classic and still comprehensive work in this regard is Robert C. Tannehill, *The Narrative Unity of Luke-Acts: A Literary Interpretation*, vol. 2: *The Acts of the Apostles* (Minneapolis: Fortress Press, 1989). In a compatible but somewhat different vein, Richard I. Pervo argues that Luke intended to be received as a work comparable to historical novels of his day, i.e., as a book that edified an audience while entertaining them. See Pervo, *Profit with Delight: The Literary Genre of the Acts of the Apostles* (Minneapolis: Fortress Press, 1987).

45. Ernst Käsemann, quoted in Ernst Haenchen, *The Acts of the Apostles: A Commentary*, trans. Bernard Noble, Gerald Shinn, and R. McL. Wilson (Oxford: Basil Blackwell, 1971), 49. See also Beverly Roberts Gaventa, "Toward a Theology of Acts: Reading and Rereading," *Interpretation* 42 (1988): 142. More recent scholarship denies the presence of early Catholicism in Acts. See Powell, What Are They Saying about Acts?, 63.

46. For example, see Donald A. McGavran and Winfield C. Arn, *Ten Steps for Church Growth* (New York: Harper & Row, 1977), who find it significant that Luke gives specific numbers of three thousand in Acts 2:41 and five thousand in Acts 4:4 when he could have simply stated that a "large number" of people heard and believed. "Specific numbers help us grasp the extent of God's blessing in the early church, even as specific goals today help focus our faith" (107).

47. Other scholars have pointed to the clear connection in the narrative between suffering and mission success, between death and the spread of the gospel. See Graham H. Twelftree, *People of the Spirit: Exploring Luke's View of the Church* (Grand Rapids: Baker Academic, 2009), 105; also Beverly Roberts Gaventa, "Aspects of Mission in the Acts of the Apostles," *Missiology* 10, no. 4 (1982): 413–25.

48. This debate was stirred by James Dunn's attempt to reclaim the New Testament concept of "baptism of the Holy Spirit" in contrast to both the Pentecostal "second blessing" and the Catholic and Protestant sacramental understanding of water baptism. He argues that the role of the Holy Spirit in both Lukan and Pauline theology is soteriological, effecting a conversion that brings individuals to faith through repentance. Against Dunn, many Pentecostal scholars posit a more "unique" Lukan pneumatology that views the role of the Spirit in missiological categories (especially emphasizing the prophetic function of the Holy Spirit to inspire speech). For the soteriological position, see Dunn, *Baptism in the Holy Spirit: A Re-Examination of the New Testament Teaching on the Gift of the Holy Spirit in Relation to Pentecostalism Today,* Studies in Biblical Theology, Second Series, 15 (London: SCM, 1970). For a strict missiological position, see Robert P. Menzies, *The Development of Early Christian Pneumatology with Special Reference to Luke-Acts,* Journal for the Study of the New Testament Supplement Series [hereafter JSNTSup] 54 (Sheffield: Sheffield Academic Press, 1991). For a mediating position, see Max B. Turner, *Power from on High: The Spirit in Israel's Restoration and Witness in Luke-Acts* (Sheffield: Sheffield Academic Press, 1996).

49. William H. Shepherd Jr., *The Narrative Function of the Holy Spirit as a Character in Luke-Acts*, Society of Biblical Literature Dissertation Series 147 (Atlanta: Scholars, 1994).

50. Ibid., 108–13.

51. Ju Hur, *A Dynamic Reading of the Holy Spirit in Acts*, JSNTSup 211 (Sheffield: Sheffield Academic Press, 2001), 31.

52. Ibid., 72–73.

53. Ibid., 185–86.

54. See Gaventa, "Aspects of Mission," 416.

55. Hur, 151, 153.

56. See n.48, above.

57. Powell, *What Are They Saying about Acts?*, 53.

58. In a number of places in Luke-Acts (Luke 1:33, 54, 68-79; 2:25, 32, 38; 24:21; Acts 3:19-21), Luke appears to look forward to a time when Israel will be restored. Scholars are divided on whether Luke sees this as an event that happened in history, a purely future event, or—as I prefer—an inbreaking eschatological event. See David Ravens, *Luke and the Restoration of Israel*, JSNTSup 119, ed. Stanley E. Porter (Sheffield: Sheffield Academic Press, 1995), 20.

59. See Wilf Hildebrandt, *An Old Testament Theology of the Spirit of God* (Peabody, MA: Hendrickson, 1995), 91–103; Wonsuk Ma, *Until the Spirit Comes: The Spirit of God in the Book of Isaiah*, Journal for the Study of the Old Testament Supplement Series 271, ed. David J. A. Clines and Philip R. Davies (Sheffield: Sheffield Academic Press, 1999).

60. Ma, *Until the Spirit Comes*, 86. Ma notes that there is also a "missionary" aspect to Israel's restoration, as seen for example in Isa. 49:6, where God promises "to raise up the tribes of Jacob and to restore the preserved of Israel; I will give you as a light to the nations, that my salvation may reach to the end of the earth" (104).

61. Hans Walter Wolff, *Joel and Amos*, trans. by Waldemar Janze, S. Dean McBride Jr., and Charles Muenchow, Hermeneia (Philadelphia: Fortress Press, 1977), 66.

62. Ibid., 67.

63. Salvation in Luke is closely linked with the forgiveness of sins; eight of the eleven New Testament references to forgiveness are in Luke's Gospel. The reference to the crowd being "cut to the heart" (2:37-38) could be read as an allusion to the new heart promised by Ezekiel and Jeremiah.

64. Twelftree, *People of the Spirit*, 82.

65. Bolt, "Mission and Witness," 193.

66. John Reumann, "*Koinonia* in Scripture: Survey of Biblical Texts," in *On the Way to Fuller Koinonia: Official Report of the Fifth World Conference on Faith and Order, Santiago de Compostela 1993*, Faith and Order Paper No. 166, ed. Thomas F. Best and Güther Gassmann (Geneva: WCC, 1993), 51.

67. Luke Timothy Johnson, *The Acts of the Apostles*, Sacra Pagina 5, ed. Daniel J. Harrington (Collegeville, MN: Liturgical, 1992), 92.

68. Douglas John Hall, *Has the Church a Future?* (Philadelphia: Westminster, 1980), 54–55.

69. As Alan Hilton writes, "The premise of other-interested life and conduct is the central identifying characteristic of Christianity, embedded in the primal narratives of creation and cross." Hilton, "Who Are We?," 154.

70. Bolt, "Mission and Witness," 197.

71. The language Luke uses in these three passages to describe the Spirit's coming ("fall upon," *epipiptō*, in 8:16; 10:44; "received," *lambanō*, in 8:17, 10:47, 19:2; and "poured out," *ekcheō*, in 10:45) echoes that of the Pentecost event (2:33, 38). See Earl Richard, "Pentecost as a Recurrent Theme in Luke-Acts," in *New Views in Luke-Acts*, ed. Earl Richard (Collegeville, MN: Liturgical, 1990), 13–49.

72. See n.48, above.

73. Johnson, *Acts of the Apostles*, 151.

74. Jacob Jervell, "The Lost Sheep of the House of Israel," in *Luke and the People of God: A New Look at Luke-Acts* (Minneapolis: Augsburg, 1972), 117–27.

75. Ravens, *Luke and the Restoration of Israel,* 99.

76. Ibid., 97.

77. Ibid., 106.

78. The story of Cornelius is told in three separate places, highlighting its significance for Luke's narrative; it also has the strongest ties to the Pentecost account in Acts 2 (10:47; 11:17; 15:8).

79. Brian S. Rosner, "The Progress of the Word," in Marshall and Peterson, eds., *Witness to the Gospel,* 227.

80. Shepherd, *Narrative Function,* 227.

81. Ibid, 229.

82. See the introduction above, 3–4.

6

An Ecclesiology That "Starts with the Spirit"

The Ecumenical Creeds

In the previous chapter, I outlined my proposal for a narrative ecclesiology that starts with the Spirit following the "story of the church" in the Acts of the Apostles. Here I apply this same method to the two ecumenical creeds of the church: the Apostles' and Nicene Creeds. In the order of both creeds, the Spirit and the church both appear in the "Third Article" and the church comes after the Holy Spirit, suggesting that ecclesiology should be rooted in the "Third Article" and "start with the Spirit."[1] In this, I follow Edmund Schlink, who proposed that within the trinitarian context of the creeds, "one should expound the doctrine of the church as the *opus propium* [proper work] of the Holy Ghost."[2]

Although many Protestants historically have been wary of grounding ecclesiology in pneumatology, Martin Luther himself seemed not to be. His explanation of the Third Article of the Apostles' Creed in his Large Catechism follows a narrative structure,[3] drawing out the story of salvation in which the Holy Spirit acts as the character who enables the church to live out the new life given in Christ's resurrection as "the communion of saints" in the "forgiveness of sins." When read as Spirit-breathed attributes, the classic "marks of the church" (one, holy, catholic, and apostolic) in the other historic ecumenical creed (the Nicean-Constantinopolitan; i.e., Nicene) help to further flesh out the church's narrative identity and purpose in a post–Christendom context.

A Theological Argument for "Starting with the Spirit"

In spite of the fact that, as Schlink stated, the Third Article of the creeds is the logical place from which to engage the question of the church, pneumatology continues to be overlooked by so many theologians from Reformation traditions, and specifically those who wish to propose a missional ecclesiology. Miroslav Volf and Maurice Lee attribute the underdevelopment of the pneumatological aspect of ecclesiology to Western theology's tendency to filter claims about the Holy Spirit christologically, by which the "Spirit guards a certain kind of relation between Christ and the church rather than directly and independently of Christ, giving concrete content to the identity and mission of the church."[4] As we saw in chapter 2, in much of traditional Protestantism the Spirit's role in ecclesiology has been understood as the application of the work of Christ to believers through a subjective appropriation of faith. The Spirit works through the preaching of the word to bring people to faith and to empower them for service in Jesus' name.[5]

A related reason that pneumatology is not often considered a starting point for ecclesiology (even missional ecclesiology) is in reaction to the tendency of some to appeal to the Spirit apart from Christ and the church. These theologians make the primary connection between the Spirit and creation (and human culture) by following the general or ecumenical interpretation of *missio Dei* as God's mission in the world.[6] For example, according to John V. Taylor, the medium in which the Creator Spirit works is the evolutionary processes of creation and human development, "to lure creatures into higher degrees of consciousness and personhood."[7] The *missio Dei* (though Taylor himself does not use this term) would be understood more in terms of "continuing creation" than redemption.[8] The Spirit does not act as the "go-between" between the church and the world, but as the "go-between" that confronts "each isolated spontaneous particle with the beckoning reality of the larger whole and so compels it to relate to others in a particular way; and that it is he who at every stage lures the inert organisms forward by giving an inner awareness and recognition of the unattained."[9] Jesus is an exemplar of the life to which the Spirit calls all people, a life lived in the "extraordinary awareness of the other and self-sacrifice of the other."[10] The church is defined as any gathering of two or three who, in Jesus' name, allow themselves to be called by the Spirit in this way.

While this view offers a more active and missional understanding of the work of the Spirit than do many traditional Protestant theologies, it does so at the expense of the particularity of the Second Article of the two ecumenical creeds, which is central to their overall narrative and soteriological arc. Methodist theologian D. Lyle Dabney offers an alternative to the false dichotomy set up between a "theology of the Second Article" (normally attributed to theologians of the Reformation), and a "theology of the First

Article" (normally attributed to scholastic and neoscholastic Catholic theology, but which could also include views such as Taylor's).[11] He calls instead for a "theology of the Third Article" that begins "neither with human possibility nor impossibility as do theologians of the first and second articles, but rather with the Spirit as the possibility of God."[12] The Holy Spirit is the relational divine reality who brings redemption *and* new creation into being.

A theology of the Third Article is fully trinitarian, according to Dabney, in that it seeks "to unfold the story of the Trinitarian mission of God in the world from the perspective of the third article of the creed; indeed, it understands itself as having been taken up into that mission."[13] Finally, such a theology finds its focus in the center of the story of God's mission in the world; that is, the life, death, and resurrection of Jesus Christ. The work of the Holy Spirit is centered in Christ, but it is more than an application or appropriation of the work of Christ in the lives of individual believers. The work of the Spirit must be defined in relation to the whole Christ event in the New Testament witness. The New Testament points to the role of the Spirit not only in terms of Jesus' ministry, which is anointed by the Spirit in the event of his baptism, but also the role of the Spirit of God in raising Jesus from the dead.[14]

Although Dabney's work in pneumatology has focused primarily on the questions of methodology and Christology,[15] there are echoes in his theology of a trinitarian understanding of *missio Dei*. He states that a theology of the Third Article is "a theology of God's mission of a transforming recreation of creation, a theology of continuity in God's presence and purpose in creation and re-creation through the discontinuity of human sin and death."[16] Although he has not explored yet this question with reference to the church as the community of the Spirit, his reference to "unfolding story" suggests a narrative as the most appropriate method for such a task.

THE STORY OF THE SPIRIT-BREATHED CHURCH IN THE APOSTLES' CREED

The late Reformation historian Gottfried Krodel has argued that narrative is the appropriate category for Luther's explanation of the articles of the Apostles' Creed. In contrast to other late medieval catechisms, Luther's purpose was not to present and debate several meanings of each article, nor to offer a commentary on the text, as was commonly done. Rather, Krodel shows how, in the First Article, Luther "'narrates' the reality of the Creator's work and the reality of my existence in the context of the reality of the Creator's work, that is, *coram Deo*. Luther creates a carefully crafted story about the Creator's work and he locates me in that story."[17]

Krodel demonstrates how Luther adapts the elements of classic rhetoric to narrate this story.[18] Luther cites the text of each article as proposition and answers it with an amplification narrated as a history that Luther phrases as a "description of persons," that is, God and God's creatures. Each statement defines and expresses the reader's existence in relationship to God.[19] Further, Luther does this in such a way as to identity with the reader's daily experiences. Again using the First Article as his example, Krodel writes, "Luther expands the cited text in such a way that the description of the God of Creation, a concept quite removed from daily human life, is developed into the description of the God who creates and sustains all that exists, but especially me, and does all this for no other reason than his fatherly goodness and mercy."[20]

In a subsequent essay, Krodel offers a rhetorical study of Luther's Second Article of the creed, showing how these same elements are present in the "story" of my redemption. He points out, however, that while Luther answers questions regarding the "who" and "what" of Jesus and his death and resurrection, he leaves several questions unanswered, such as "What is the nature of Christ's lordship? How does Christ's rule function? Where is Christ's kingdom? How or by what means am I able to say, 'Jesus is my Lord?' . . . How can this story become my own story?" While this appears to be a lacuna in Luther's story, it is really a bridge that connects the Second Article with the Third Article, leading the reader from Christology to pneumatology and ecclesiology.[21]

Most Lutheran treatments of Luther's "Third-Article theology" have focused on the personal aspect of the Holy Spirit's work to "make this story *my* story." For example, Jeffrey Mann has argued that the "proper work" of the Holy Spirit is to bring the believer to faith.[22] For German Lutheran theologian Eilert Herms, it is the task of the Holy Spirit to represent the past and future acts of God to the believer; otherwise, the redeeming work of the incarnate Son of God on the cross would remain hidden and unknown, and therefore lost. The Holy Spirit works externally through the preaching of the word and internally in the human heart, to bring this revelation to each believer. This revelatory work of the Holy Spirit also can be identified as the Spirit's sanctifying work because the revelation of the meaning and truth of the gospel into each believer's heart itself brings an existential transformation to the believer and a new eschatological standing before God.[23] Thus the work of the Holy Spirit is sanctifying in that it endows each human person with self-certainty about her or his redemption.[24] Forgiveness of sins is also understood as a revelatory experience, as "nothing other than recreated existence in light of the appearance of the truth of the gospel."[25]

However, the "characters" in the Third Article of the creed include not only the Holy Spirit and the individual believer, but also the church. Although Herms does not devote a particular subsection to the church in his book,[26] he does recognize the necessity of the church for the proclamation of the gospel, through which the Holy Spirit reveals the truth of the cross.[27] Further, he understands that believers are simultaneously incorporated into the body of Christ when they are existentially transformed.[28] However, Herms' treatment of Luther's pneumatology fails to explore in any depth the communal implications of Luther's view of sanctification. For Luther, the church is more than an instrument or "means of grace" through which the Holy Spirit sanctifies believers. Luther draws out a mutual relationship between the individual and community often overlooked in this regard, whereby sanctification itself is not only an individual and personal event, but one that is also relational and communal. It is in community that God's "holy people" corporately lives out and experiences the new existence given through Christ and the Spirit, until the day of resurrection.

A close reading of the Large Catechism will help illustrate this point. In his introduction to his explanation of the Third Article, Luther calls the Holy Spirit the Sanctifier, the one who makes us holy, and states that the point of this article is sanctification (paras. 34–37). The rest of his explanation can be split into three sections, whereby Luther speaks of the Holy Spirit effecting our "being made holy" through (1) the community of saints or the Christian church; (2) the forgiveness of sins; and (3) the resurrection of the body and life everlasting.

1. *The Holy Spirit effects our being made holy through the community of saints.*[29] In this first section, Luther does emphasize the role of the Holy Spirit and the church in the process by which individual believers are "called through the gospel." He writes, "The Spirit first leads us into his holy community, placing us in the church's lap, where he preaches to us *and brings us to Christ.*"[30] The personal language in this section describing the Spirit's relationship to the believer is striking. He reiterates: "Being made holy is nothing else than bringing us to the Lord Jesus Christ to receive this blessing [the redemption won for us by Christ on the cross], to which we could not have come by ourselves."[31] Luther goes on to speak of the church as well in personal terms, as the "mother" who begets and bears each Christian through the word, that is, a community of new birth.[32]

Here Luther describes holiness in terms of the gift of faith, that is, a knowledge and understanding in believers' hearts of the benefits won by Christ for believers. The Holy Spirit reveals and proclaims the word of God, "through which he illuminates and inflames hearts so that they grasp and accept it, cling to it and persevere in it."[33] As we saw, this is the role that Herms and some other Lutherans tend to emphasize in Luther's pneumatology. Luther does not stop there, however. He goes on to emphasize the communal aspect of this new life that Christians receive through Christ by the power of the Holy Spirit.[34] Believers are also brought into his body, into the assembly of saints, a holy community.[35] The proclamation that brings the good news to each individual believer is not only a revelatory experience. Each believer is simultaneously incorporated into the holy community *in order to become* "a part and member, a participant and co-partner in all the blessings it possesses."[36] Luther calls this community a "holy little flock" that the Spirit gathers in one faith, mind, and understanding, under the headship of Christ. The holy community "possesses a variety of gifts, and yet is united in love without sect or schism." It grows daily and becomes strong in the faith and "in its fruits," which the Spirit produces.[37] The holy community is not simply instrumental to the Spirit's work of preaching the word and creating faith. In other words, believers not only receive the promise of new life, but also a new community in which to begin living out this promise.

2. *The Holy Spirit effects our being made holy through the forgiveness of sins.* The primary blessing believers receive in the holy community is the daily forgiveness of sins, which they obtain through word and sacrament. Believers need forgiveness continually, because they are never without sin in this life. This blessing is not only experienced vertically, between the individual believer and God, but also horizontally, that is, communally and relationally with other believers. As Luther writes, the Christian experiences new life as "full forgiveness of sins, both in that God forgives us *and that we forgive, bear with, and aid one another.*"[38] Holiness is brought about by the gospel and the forgiveness of sins; indeed, for Luther, holiness is dependent on the daily experience of the forgiveness of sins—and not moral perfection. In fact, Luther states, "All who would seek to merit holiness through their works rather than the gospel and the forgiveness of sins" separate themselves from the holy community.[39] Holiness is described as new life experienced in terms of faith and forgiveness of sins, given through the gospel and the Spirit. This gift is always received from outside of the believing community (through the encounter of Christ in the word), but is experienced daily within the community through the power of the Holy Spirit.

3. *The Holy Spirit effects our being made holy through the resurrection of the body and the life everlasting.* In this final section, Luther speaks of the growth of the holy community in eschatological terms. Holiness has begun and is growing daily, but "now we remain only halfway pure and holy."[40] The Holy Spirit will continue to work in us, increasing holiness on the earth through the church and the forgiveness, until the last day, when there are only perfectly pure and holy people. That is, God will continue to increase faith, forgiveness of sins, and the fruits of the Spirit in the church during its earthly pilgrimage as God's "holy flock," so that it may bear the blessings it has received from Christ, for the sake of the world. As Luther states, "The Holy Spirit continues his work without ceasing until the Last Day, and *for this purpose he has appointed a community on earth, through which he speaks and does all of his work.* For he has not yet gathered together all of this Christian community, nor has he completed the granting of forgiveness."[41] The Holy Spirit not only speaks *to* the holy community, but *through* the holy community to extend God's blessings to the world.

Luther's own "theology of the Third Article" offers a starting point for a narrative, missional ecclesiology for mainline churches today, especially those with Reformation roots. In his explanation of the Apostles' Creed, Luther offers a "description of persons" and their actions in the story of salvation. The Holy Spirit and the people of God are the characters in this chapter of the story, a narrative that is as personal as it is cosmic in scope. This story arc is outlined in the Third Article of the Apostles' Creed and driven by the third person of the Trinity, the Holy Spirit, beginning with the new life of the resurrection and Pentecost events and ending with the promise of Christ's second coming. Returning to Luther's explanation of the Third Article of the creed in the Large Catechism with Krodel's narrative method as a framework, we see that the church is a Spirit-breathed church, a church whose identity and purpose are given and empowered by the the Holy Spirit orienting the believers to the gospel. The story of our salvation begins with the Holy Spirit orienting believers to the gospel, and incorporating them into a "holy community" as a people brought into communion with God (and each other) through the power of the Holy Spirit. The church lives out the story of its Spirit-breathed communion through the community of relationships marked by the communication (and experience) of the forgiveness of sins, a gift first received and continually promised through the Holy Spirit. As the church shares the gift of forgiveness and the fruits of the Holy Spirit with one another, the church is inspired, led, and sent by the Holy Spirit to live in anticipation of its final destiny in the kingdom of God, living in the new life given to it in the resurrection as "the communion of saints," living in "the forgiveness of sins."

This identity is reflected not only in the creation of this community (the church as "creature of the word") but also in the ongoing life of this community, ruled by the power of the Holy Spirit who lives out its new existence in faith and in the experience of forgiveness, not only personally and existentially, but also relationally and communally (the church as "communion"). The Holy Spirit gives the church its narrative identity as a Spirit-breathed people, in whom the Spirit breathes new life, life that is experienced not only existentially through the gift of faith but also through the lived-out reality of forgiveness of sins and transformed relationships. This is a community that grows in "holiness," because the Holy Spirit is at work within and through its members. This community can be be recognized not only by its "holy possessions" (the means of grace) but also by the new life shared within itself, as the Holy Spirit enables members to forgive one another and live peaceably with one another. This "embodied holiness" itself becomes a witness to the world (the missional church).

A Pneumatology of the Cross?

D. Lyle Dabney has leveled an important critique against Luther as a theologian of the cross. Dabney argues that Luther has failed to root his account of the Spirit in the cross. For Dabney, to know who the Holy Spirit is, one must return to the "center of the story"—the cross of Jesus Christ—and reclaim the *theologia crucis* as a *theologia pneuma*. While Luther defines the Holy Spirit formally as the third person of the Trinity, he defines the Spirit materially in anthropological terms; that is, the Spirit is the one who "makes us holy."[42] Dabney thus charges that, for Luther, the work of the Spirit is thus articulated in the present tense and "certainly [is] not oriented to the cross and certainly not to 'humiliation and shame' but rather to community and forgiveness and resurrection and new life."[43] Dabney attributes this weakness in Luther, which he argues is shared by all the Reformers, to a subordination of the Spirit to the Son, whereby the work of the Spirit is understood as subjectively applying the objective benefits of the cross to the believer through faith. With Volf and Lee, Dabney argues that the solution is found through a consideration of the work of the Spirit from the "other side" of the relationship between the Spirit and the Son, in particular, the role of the Holy Spirit in Jesus' incarnation, his earthly mission, his suffering, crucifixion, and resurrection.

If we read Luther's explanation of the Apostles' Creed in the narrative framework as suggested by Gottfried Krodel, however, Dabney's critique of Luther seems somewhat misplaced.[44] Luther presents his explanation of the

Apostles' Creed as a narrative soteriology *pro me*, not as a systematic theology of the Trinity. Luther's explanation of the Second Article, though focused on the past tense event of the cross, is also articulated in present, personal, salvific terms. In personalizing the event of the cross "for us and our redemption," it does not follow that Luther thereby subordinates his Christology to anthropology, as Dabney accuses Luther of doing with his pneumatology. As Christoph Schwöbel notes, by reorganizing the Apostles' Creed into three rather than twelve articles, Luther purports the integration of a series of formerly independent articles of belief in the church, so that "the Spirit's work of sanctification is now not only related to a particular aspect of the doctrine of grace; it now comprises the whole dynamic of God's Trinitarian action. The Spirit thus becomes the common denominator of ecclesiology, soteriology and eschatology."[45]

Further, one also could argue that at the center of the cross—and Jesus' own experience of the cross—was not only the pain and shame of his suffering, but also the liberating power of forgiveness and reconciliation. The Lukan narrative, rather than recording Jesus' painful cry of abandonment, has Jesus speak a reconciling word from the cross: "Father, forgive them; for they do not know what they are doing" (Luke 23:34). Through the resurrection, this word becomes available to all who believe in him. As noted in the previous chapter, both Luke and John connect the coming of the Holy Spirit (Acts 2; John 20) with the forgiveness of sins. Thus the gift of forgiveness itself flows from the event of the cross and resurrection. The Spirit who raised Jesus from the dead becomes the agent of this new life in the believers, a new life experienced in the present but which finds its eschatological fulfillment in the promised parousia.

Luther's explanation of the Third Article, although referring to the event of the cross in the past tense and the work of the Spirit in the present tense, connects these two events in a larger narrative framework. The Spirit is the "character" who in this narrative "brings us to Christ" (which for Luther always meant the crucified Christ). The people are brought to Christ in order to be forgiven and to receive new life and salvation, because, as Luther insists in the Small Catechism, "where there is forgiveness of sins, there is also life and salvation."[46] As forgiveness is received, it is simultaneously shared and communicated to others; believers are forgiven and enabled to forgive others, through the reconciling work of the Holy Spirit. In this sense, one can say that justification belongs to the Third Article, as Dabney himself argues elsewhere, "According to the witness of the New Testament, Christ has come not simply to convey a new status upon the dying but rather to reconcile those who are dead in trespasses and sin to the living God through a renewed gift of life in resurrection, and in doing so, to bring forth the new out of the old and thus create creation anew."[47] The agent of new life—from the very beginning to the end—is the Spirit of life.[48]

Dabney rightly argues that an exclusive use of traditional forensic metaphors cannot do justice to the reconciling work of God in the cross of Jesus Christ. Rather than speak of "a forensic act of 'gracious exclusion,' as one Reformed theologian has termed it, *Christus extra nos* and *Christus pro nobis*," we need to speak, rather, of "God's acts of gracious inclusion in the life of the resurrecting Spirit of God who incorporates us into the life and death and resurrection of Jesus Christ our Lord."[49] What I wish to add to Dabney's point is that this incorporation happens as we are made members of the body of Christ, the community of the Spirit.[50] This is a reconciliation that is experienced relationally, as Dabney himself insists when he states, "The tale of human sin and divine redemption is told in relational and not in ontological categories in the biblical witness."[51] In Dabney's schema, however, the individual—albeit relationally defined—rather than the new spiritual community remains the locus for God's reconciling work. The missing piece in Dabney's account of a theology of the Third Article is ecclesiology!

Following Luther's narrative framework, the work of the Holy Spirit is not only to appropriate faith subjectively to the believer but, as the person of the Trinity who initiates our relationship with God in Christ and our relationships with each other as members of Christ's body, the Spirit also brings us to the crucified Christ to receive forgiveness, life, and salvation. Indeed, Dabney suggests that we conceive of the Spirit as "*trans*jective," that is to say, "that by which we as individuals are transcended, engaged, oriented beyond ourselves and related to God and neighbor from the very beginning."[52] Likewise, the spiritual community does not possess the Holy Spirit, but is possessed *by* it. Sanctification happens *in* the spiritual community, as the Holy Spirit makes of us a community, holy through the living out of relationships in forgiveness of sins. The Spirit is the one who relates us to God (which we appropriate by faith/trust) and to each other (which we appropriate in loving, forgiving relationships). Even as Luther speaks of the transformative power of the Spirit who causes the spiritual community to grow, the Lutheran and Reformed concern for the alien nature of the righteousness of Christ is retained, because this growth happens not as an internal growth of infused grace, but *extra nos* (outside of ourselves) through the forgiveness of sins experienced in the community through relationships.

The Attributes of the Spirit-Breathed Church in the Nicene Creed

In this section, I examine the classic "marks of the church" (one, holy, catholic, and apostolic) in the other historic catholic creed—the Niceo-Constantinopolitan, or Nicene, Creed—in light of the church's narrative that has been sketched out in Acts and the Apostles' Creed. These marks, which have long been used to define the nature of the church, will be explored here as attributes of the Spirit-breathed church's narrative and missional identity for a post-Christendom context. For Protestants in the Reformation tradition, the "marks of the church" more typically refer to word and sacrament (and for some, discipline) rather than the four "notes" that appear in the Nicene Creed, because of how the creedal marks were used by Counter-Reformation apologists. They were treated as distinguishing characteristics, recognizable marks, by which the true church can be perceived apart from false claimants.[53] Of course, the apologists understood these marks to be firmly and visibly rooted and guaranteed by the ecclesial structures of the church, the office of bishop, the papacy, canon law, and so forth.[54] The Reformers had no objection to the classic attributes of the church, but they rejected the idea that they could be empirically identified by these ecclesial structures. The only outward signs by which they claimed one can discern the true church were the pure proclamation of the word and the administration of the sacraments in accordance with the institution of Christ.

For Christians rooted in the Reformation tradition, then, the four adjectives in the creed cannot serve as marks or notes in the determinative sense. As we saw in chapter 2, for Luther and Calvin the church's identity is constituted and marked by the event of the word being proclaimed and the sacraments being administered. One cannot point to anything except these means of grace to know "where" the church is. The church is created by the word and sacrament but it is the Spirit that works through these means to shape a people for ministry and mission. Even if they cannot be objectively verifiable tests of a church's authenticity, we do well to consider them as "serious points of corporate reflection, part of that process of critical self-examination that belongs to the household of faith."[55] If we understand these marks as the Reformers did—as attributes or dimensions[56] of the church—they can assist the mainline churches in North America in addressing the crisis in which they find themselves, which I have argued is an identity crisis. Further, if we view these notes of the church as dimensions of the Spirit's activity in and amidst this "holy community," they can help us think about the church's Spirit-breathed identity and purpose or mission in the world today. As dimensions of the Spirit's activity, these "notes" are first of all reflective of the God who calls the church into being:

> 1. One—"that they may be one, as we are one, I in them and you in me, that they become completely one so that the world may believe" (John 17:22).
> 2. Holy—"You shall be holy, for I am holy" (1 Peter 15).
> 3. Catholic—"For in him the whole fullness of deity dwells bodily, and you have come to fullness in him, who is the head of every ruler and authority" (Col. 2:9).[57]
> 4. Apostolic—"As the Father has sent me, so I send you . . . Receive the Holy Spirit" (John 20:21-22).

Although unity may seem to have a logical priority and to be the most obvious starting point for an American ecclesiology, considering the sheer number of denominations in the United States, I am going to suggest that we begin in reverse order for three reasons, two theological and one contextual. If we begin our consideration of the marks of the church with the attribute of unity as a reflection of the perichoretic unity of the Trinity, we risk an idealized concept of the church, the dangers of which I discussed already in chapter 3. As Stephen Bevans and others remind us, what is first in our knowledge of the triune nature is not the perichoretic union of the three persons of the Trinity but, rather, "the divine missions of Word and Spirit, which in turn ground our knowledge of the processions and persons of the Trinity."[58] To begin with the divine missions of word and Spirit suggests beginning with the mark of apostolicity, with the "sentness" of God's own self in the incarnation and Pentecost, and God's sending of the church into the world to bear God's love. Moreover, from a specifically Reformation perspective, it makes sense to begin with apostolicity, since it is the mark that refers to the teaching of the apostles, the message of the gospel, the *kergyma*. According to Luther and Calvin, it is the proclamation of this gospel message in word and sacrament that creates the church.[59]

A final reason for starting with apostolicity is contextual. If we understand that the mainline churches in America are in need of a "missional ecclesiology," it makes eminent sense to begin with this dimension of the church. Here I follow Darrell Guder and the Gospel and Our Culture Network, who propose that we read and understand the Nicene marks in reverse order "in order to restore missional purpose to our theology of the church. . . . It is a simple and yet revolutionary proposal: What if we were to say that the church we confess is apostolic, catholic, holy, and therefore one? . . . If we start our Nicene ecclesiology with apostolicity, then we end up defining catholicity and holiness and oneness in rather different ways—in ways closer to the sequence of formation that we find in the Biblical documents."[60]

APOSTOLIC

Apostolicity is customarily defined as continuity with and faithfulness to the apostolic tradition.[61] As crucial as it is to stress the apostolic origins of the gospel message, Carl Braaten reminds us that it does not mean "constructing an irreducible minimum of apostolic doctrines, nor does it mean linking into an unbroken chain of apostolic offices of leadership; it does mean laying hold of the original eschatological drive of the early Christian apostolate and tracing its trajectory through the discontinuities of time and history."[62] As a pneumatological dimension of the church's identity, apostolicity also must be understood in the original New Testament sense of being sent out to bear witness to the eschatological future that has broken forth in the life, death, and resurrection of Jesus Christ. Indeed, when we hear "apostolic," we should think "missional." As we saw in chapter 5, the Holy Spirit blows on the disciples, turning them from fear to bold proclamation of the new life of the resurrection. It is the Holy Spirit who serves as the church's "mission director," turning disciples into apostles, so that the gospel may be proclaimed to the ends of the earth. And as Luther reminds us, because the Holy Spirit has not yet gathered together all of God's people, nor has completed the granting of forgiveness, the church has been appointed as the community through which the Spirit speaks and does its work.[63]

The mainline churches in North America need to reclaim this dimension of their ecclesial identity. Because of the legacy of *de facto* Christendom, most congregations do not see themselves first and foremost as communities commissioned and authorized sent out by the Holy Spirit to witness to God's liberating good news. This attribute reminds the church that it is not a community called by God in order to "bless" the culture or to serve as a social club for its own "members," but to be sent out into neighborhoods and communities in order to witness to the power of the resurrection to bring new life individually and communally.

CATHOLIC

A church can only be apostolic if it is also catholic, because the scope of the apostolic mission is total and universal. Protestants with Reformation roots have not always been comfortable with this term because of its association with obedience to Rome. Following Augustine, the "catholic church" was defined as the universal church spread throughout the world whose unity is manifested under the authority of Rome.[64] Substituting "Christian" for "catholic" does not add anything, however, since "there can be no question of any other church in the Third Article of the Creed than the Christian church."[65] More common today is the substitution of the word *universal*, which comes closer but still does not capture the full meaning of the term *catholic*. The word in the original Greek is *kata holon*, which means "according to or appropriate to the whole."

In 1968, the Fourth Assembly of the World Council of Churches in Uppsala defined catholicity as "the quality by which the church expresses the fullness, the integrity, and the totality of life in Christ." For Edmund Schlink, "this means that the concept of catholicity is understood in the light of the rich variety of the Spirit's gifts, and, at the same time, of the service to the world which the Spirit inspires."[66] Instead of simply identifying this Spirit-breathed attribute of the church with the universal scope of the apostolic mission (although it includes that), one might say with Darrell Guder that "the catholicity of the church is demonstrated in all the ways that the church at every level witnesses to the one gospel that draws all people to Christ."[67] In other words, this attribute is qualitative as well as quantitative. A "catholic" church is one that allows itself to be blown by the Spirit beyond the limits of particularity in order to embrace the world in all of its rich diversity—as the church in the book of Acts did. It is the ecclesiastical word for what is meant by "inclusive."

To be catholic means consciously to point beyond one's own particular ecclesial community to the global church as a fuller expression of the Spirit's work in creating and shaping a people.[68] This is more than recognizing that each local congregation is a part of a larger ecclesial whole. To say that the church is catholic is not just to say that our congregation is in communion with other congregations throughout the world, but that this communion extends to all classes and kinds of people. As a catholic community, the church is called to be all-embracing in how *and to whom* it reaches out in mission, reflecting the fullness of Christ and the universal redemption available through his life, death, and resurrection.

Such a catholic identity suggests the need to call into question the self-interests of members and groups within the church at every level, especially the local congregation.[69] In this sense, the disestablishment of the mainline Protestant churches in the United States from positions of influence and hegemony offers a real opportunity to reclaim true catholicity as a dimension of the church's Spirit-breathed identity. For the mainline churches in North America, this includes rejecting all attempts to define their own cultural tradition or theology as normative for the global church.[70] Specifically for many Lutheran congregations in the United States, this challenges the historical ethnic enclaves and tendency toward social and classist parochialism. In order to claim the ecclesial dimension of catholicity, white Lutherans and other mainline Protestants in North America need to own up to this parochialism and the privilege that comes with having white skin, and to acknowledge more honestly the racist heritage of our country, including the legacy and continuing impact of slavery and Jim Crow, the taking of Native American lands, and unfair government housing policies and immigration practices. The church has an opportunity to bring the gospel of reconciliation to these issues, but it cannot do so without helping Americans first name the sin and violence that has marred our country in so many racialized ways.[71]

HOLY

The church is called to be apostolic, to witness to the good news of Jesus Christ and the eschatological future he brings, in which "all belong to the whole" in the fullness of life in his name that is offered through the Holy Spirit. In order to witness to this inbreaking future, the church is called to be "holy." This may be the most misunderstood of the attributes or dimensions of the church's Spirit-breathed identity. First, holiness must be understood as being "set apart" for this mission in order to engage the world, not to withdraw from it. As with the other attributes, holiness is not an empirical designation that is observable by looking at, in this case, the piety of its members. As we saw in Luther's explanation of the Third Article of the creed, holiness is the result of the Holy Spirit working in and through the church to reconcile and heal with the forgiveness of sins given through Jesus Christ. This dimension of ecclesial identity needs to be reclaimed as an attribute of the whole church, not just of its individual members. Too often, holiness in the North American experience, from the two Great Awakenings to more recent revival movements, has been defined in individualistic (focusing on personal salvation and sanctification) and moralistic (with a particular concern for sexual purity) terms.

The apostolic mission of the church includes not only proclaiming to others the forgiveness and reconciliation given in Jesus Christ, but learning to live by the power of forgiveness in its own relationships—even if imperfectly. As we recall, for Luther the "full forgiveness of sins" is that "God forgives us and that we forgive, bear with and aid one another."[72] Too often the church's proclamation of the gospel is hampered by its lack of living according to the same. Many people "outside of the church's four walls" are seeking what the church purports to have—authentic community, healing, and reconciliation—but when they walk into the typical mainline congregation, they find instead a social club where members are bickering about unimportant things, people who not only refuse to live by forgiveness, but instead hold grudges and carry resentments. When I was serving as a pastor, I learned that the main reason someone left a congregation was not because of doctrinal differences with the denomination or the pastor, but because of a conflict that festered into resentment or turned into an outright fight. Feelings were hurt and reconciliation was never broached or attempted, and inevitably, the hurt party would stop attending church altogether. It is true that the church itself is *simul iustus et peccator*—that is, at the same time a fellowship of sinners and a fellowship of saints—and yet, as Luther reminds us, the Holy Spirit is always present to heal and to forgive, making the church "holy," so that it may demonstrate the inbreaking and gracious rule of God and be an instrument of God's sanctifying and gracious rule for others.[73]

UNITY

As Jesus himself prays in his high priestly prayer in John 17:20-21, unity ought to serve the mission of the church: "I ask not only on behalf of these, but also on behalf of those who will believe in me through their word, that they may all be one. As you, Father, are in me and I am in you, may they also be in us, so that the world may believe that you have sent me." The lack of visible unity among the churches remains a serious obstacle to the church's identity and mission as a Spirit-breathed people. While Christians already share spiritual unity through their baptism into Christ and faith, the healing of historic divisions in the church enables the church to experience this *koinonia* in more and deeper ways and to be a more effective witness in the world. Ecumenism does not create unity, but it gives visible expression to the spiritual unity and *koinonia* that already exists among the baptized in the one body of Christ.

As is well known, the history of Protestant Christianity in the United States has been one of division and merger. In addition to the divisions that immigrant Christians brought with them when they came to America, Christians in the United States have split over various doctrinal and ethical issues, including slavery. Mainline denominations, including my own ELCA, are committed to ecumenical dialogue to heal historic breaches and theological differences that have marked the past. In six cases, this has led to entering into a "full communion" relationship with another denomination (The Episcopal Church, the Presbyterian Church–USA, the Reformed Church of America, the United

Church of Christ, the Moravian Church, and the United Methodist Church), In another case, it led to a public service of repentance and healing (with Mennonites). As stated in its constitution, the ELCA seeks in its faith and life "to manifest the unity given to the people of God by living together in the love of Christ and by joining with other Christians in prayer and action to express and preserve the unity which the Spirit gives" (ELCA Constitution 4.02.f.). In order to express more visibly the "unity which the Spirit gives," a Spirit-breathed church will not be afraid to address both the theological differences that have historically divided our denominations and the issues that continue to further divide Christians within denominations (e.g., sexuality, biblical interpretation), as well as the fact that American Christians continue to segregate themselves by race and class.

CONCLUSION

For too long, many Protestants have avoided or disregarded the relationship between the Spirit and the church in ecclesiological formations. A narrative ecclesiology that "starts with the Spirit" offers fresh perspectives on the question, "Who is the church?" The narrative identity of the church can be traced not only through the Scriptures, especially the Acts of the Apostles, but also the historic creeds of the church. These accessible resources can aid pastors and other church leaders struggling to address the identity crisis of the church in a post-Christendom context. The epilogue below will suggest some ways that such leaders might apply these constructive ideas in the life and ministry of concrete congregations.

FOR REFLECTION AND DISCUSSION

1. What are some of the reasons pneumatology has not been considered as a starting point for ecclesiology, especially by Protestants? What does D. Lyle Dabney propose in response to these concerns?

2. Have you ever thought about the Apostles' Creed in narrative terms? How does Martin Luther narrate the events of salvation in his explanation of the creed in his Large Catechism?

3. What can we learn about the identity and mission of the church today from Luther's "story of the church" in his explanation of the Third Article of the creed? What connections can be found between his narrative rendering and the Spirit-driven narrative in the Acts of the Apostles for a twenty-first-century ecclesiology?

4. Is an ecclesiology that "starts with the Spirit" automatically a "theology of glory?" What place does the cross have in a Spirit-breathed church?

5. How have the Nicene "marks" of the church (one, holy, catholic, apostolic) historically been used in ecclesiology? How does the proposal to think of them instead as "dimensions of the Spirit's activity" help you think about the church's Spirit-breathed identity and purpose or mission in the world today?

6. In what specific ways do these attributes challenge many of the operating assumptions of the idea of the church as a "voluntary association" and the corresponding "club mentality" of many mainline congregations?

Notes

1. Miroslav Volf and Maurice Lee note that the pairing of "the Spirit" with "the church" goes back to at least the third century and echoes the close ties between the Spirit and the church found throughout the New Testament. Volf and Lee, "The Spirit and the Church," in *Advents of the Spirit: An Introduction to the Current Study of Pneumatology,* ed. Bradford E. Hinze and D. Lyle Dabney (Milwaukee: Marquette University Press, 2001), 382.

2. Edmund Schlink, *The Coming Christ and the Coming Church* (Philadelphia: Fortress Press, 1968), 96.

3. In fact, George Lindbeck notes that for Luther, the creed is a summary of the gospel, "and the gospel, in turn, is narrative: it proclaims the history of God's gracious dealings with humankind in creation, the coming of Jesus Christ (the climactic part of the story), and the gathering of a people, the Church, through the Holy Spirit." See George Lindbeck, "Martin Luther and the Rabbinic Mind," in *The Church in a Postliberal Age*, ed. James J. Buckley (Grand Rapids: Eerdmans, 2002), 25.

4. Volf and Lee, "Spirit and the Church," 383.

5. For a discussion of the Protestant appropriation of pneumatology to the "subjective side" or "subjective realization" of reconciliation, see Michael Welker, *God the Spirit,* trans. John F. Hoffmeyer (Minneapolis: Fortress Press, 1994), 43–44.

6. See ch. 4, above, for discussion of this paradigm of *missio Dei.*

7. John V. Taylor, *The Go-Between God: The Holy Spirit and the Christian Mission* (New York: SCM, 1972), 33.

8. Ibid., 36.

9. Ibid., 31.

10. Ibid., 135.

11. See D. Lyle Dabney, "Why Should the First Be Last? The Priority of Pneumatology in Recent Theological Discussion," in Hinze and Dabney, eds., *Advents of the Spirit,* 240–61. See also "Otherwise Engaged in the Spirit: A First Theology for a Twenty-First Century," in *The Future of Theology: Essays in Honor of Jürgen Moltmann,* ed. Miroslav Volf, Carmen Krieg, and Thomas Kucharz (Grand Rapids: Eerdmans, 1996), 154–63.

12. Dabney, "Why Should the First Be Last?," 254.

13. Ibid., 255.

14. Ibid., 255–56.

15. See, for example, Dabney's essays in *Starting with the Spirit: Task of Theology Today II*, ed. Stephen Pickard and Gordon Preece (Hindmarsh: Australian Theological Forum, 2001).

16. Dabney, "Why Should the First be Last?," 255.

17. Gottfried G. Krodel, "Luther's Work on the Catechism in the Context of Late Medieval Catechetical Literature," *Concordia Journal* 25, no. 4 (October 1999): 380.

18. Ibid., 382.

19. Ibid., 383.

20. Ibid., 382.

21. Gottfried G. Krodel, "Luther as Creative Writer: The Explanation of the Second Article of the Apostles' Creed in the Small Catechism," in *Ad Fontes Lutheri: Toward the Recovery of the Real Luther, Essays in Honor of Kenneth Hagen's Sixty-Fifth Birthday,* ed. Timothy Maschke, Franz Posset, and Joan Skocir, Marquette Studies in Theology 28 (Milwaukee: Marquette University Press, 2001), 130–64. To my knowledge, Krodel never specifically treated Luther's explanation of the Third Article in a similar fashion.

22. Jeffrey K. Mann, "Luther and the Holy Spirit: Why Pneumatology Still Matters," *Currents in Theology and Mission* 34 (2007): 111–16. As Luther writes in the much memorized passage from the Small Catechism, "I believe that I cannot by my own understanding or strength believe in Jesus Christ my Lord or come to him, but instead the Holy Spirit has called me through the gospel, enlightened me with his gifts, made me holy, and kept me in the true faith." Martin Luther, "The Small Catechism," in *The Book of Concord: The Confessions of the Evangelical Lutheran Church*, Robert Kolb and Timothy J. Wengert, eds., trans. Charles Arand, et al. (Minneapolis: Fortress Press, 2000), 355. Hereafter, *BC*.

23. Eilert Herms, *Luthers Auslegung des Dritten Artikels* (Tübingen: J. C. B. Mohr [Paul Siebeck], 1987), 65, 100.

24. Ibid., 74.

25. Ibid., 96.

26. The topic of the church is treated in the last subsection of the chapter, "The Revelation Event as Eschatological Event," in ibid.

27. "Outside of this community of his body, there is no access to Christ." Herms, 52; English translation is mine.

28. Ibid., 110.

29. Simo Peura points out that word Luther uses is not *Gemeinschaft* ("community") but *Gemeine*, which is perhaps closer to the English "fellowship" or "sharing or participative community." See his discussion in "The Church as Spiritual Communion," in Heinrich Holze, ed., *The Church as Communion: Lutheran Contributions to Ecclesiology*, LWF Documentation 42 (Geneva: Lutheran World Federation, 1997), 104–21.

30. Martin Luther, "The Large Catechism," in *BC*, 435–36.

31. Ibid., 436.

32. According to Regin Prenter, Luther understood the role of the Holy Spirit as bestowing Christ on us through the word; it is only in this moment that the word becomes "God's living Word." Regin Prenter, *Spiritus Creator*, trans. John M. Jensen (Philadelphia: Muhlenberg, 1953), 106–107.

33. *BC*, 436.

34. In the second part of this first section (paras. 47–52).

35. Luther understands "communion of saints" to be a later gloss on "holy Christian church"; for him they signify the same thing. Luther discusses his preference for the term "a holy Christian people" (Ger.: *Gemeine*) rather than *ecclesia*, or *Kirche*, or even the term usually preferred by Lutherans, "assembly." *BC*, 437.

36. Ibid., 438; italics mine.

37. Ibid.

38. Ibid.; italics mine.

39. Ibid.

40. Ibid.

41. Ibid.

42. Dabney, "Naming the Spirit," in *Starting with the Spirit*, 32.

43. Ibid., 33.

44. This is not to say that Luther's account of the Spirit cannot be improved; indeed, an exploration of Spirit-Christology is well deserving of Lutheran attention. I simply wish to suggest that Luther's narrative pneumatology is richer than Dabney presents.

45. Christoph Schwöbel, "Quest for Communion," in Holze, *Church as Communion*, 273.

46. This quote comes from Luther's explanation of the Lord's Supper; see *BC*, 362.

47. Dabney, "Justification of the Spirit," in *Starting with the Spirit*, 67.

48. As Dabney points out, "According to the witness of the early church, therefore, it is the Holy Spirit, the eschatological *Spiritus Vivificans* by and in whose power Jesus Christ has been raised to new and transformed existence." Dabney, "Naming the Spirit," 41.

49. Dabney, "Justification of the Spirit." 75.

50. I use the term *members* here (and elsewhere in this book) to refer to the Pauline concept of membership in the body of Christ (1 Cor. 12:12-26), though I recognize that in the American context this term has become associated with voluntary associations. I do think that the term itself can be salvaged as long as the Pauline image is central; that is, we may speak of church members if we mean that we are members of Christ and thereby, of each other, rather than dues-paying members of an organization.

51. Ibid., 75.

52. Dabney, "The Nature of the Spirit: Creation as Premonition of God," in *Starting with the Spirit*, 101.

53. Hans Küng, *The Church*, trans. Ray and Rosaleen Ockenden (London: Burns & Oates, 1967), 266.

54. Since Vatican II, Catholic theologians largely have abandoned the apologetical approach in favor a more eschatological approach, whereby "the four marks are as much future goals of the church, still to be achieved, as they are present realities." Richard P. McBrien, "The Marks of the Church," *National Catholic Reporter*, August 8, 2008, http://www.rpinet.com/wforum/index.php?t=tree&th=3566&rid=0&S=3fdde5a01604b94edc455a8d5167a81f.

55. Douglas John Hall, *Confessing the Faith: Christian Theology in a North American Context* (Minneapolis: Fortress Press, 1996), 72.

56. Hans Küng's preferred term for the traditional marks. See Küng, *The Church*, 8.

57. Avery Dulles suggests that the term *plēroma* ("fullness") is perhaps the nearest biblical equivalent for what we call catholicity. Dulles, *The Catholicity of the Church* (Oxford: Clarendon, 1985), 31.

58. Neil Ormerod, "The Structure of a Systematic Ecclesiology," *Theological Studies* 63 (2002): 29. See also Stephen Bevans, "God Inside Out: Notes toward a Missionary Theology of the Spirit," *International Bulletin of Missionary Research* 22, no. 3 (1998): 102–105.

59. According to Edmund P. Clowney, "The marks of the church, as developed during the Protestant Reformation, centered on the church as apostolic. The sure sign of Christ's true church is the preaching of the apostolic gospel." Clowney, *The Church* (Downers Grove, IL: InterVarsity, 1995), 73.

60. Darrell L. Guder, "The Nicene Marks in a Post-Christendom Church," unpublished paper, 27 December 2005, 9–10, http://www.pcusa.org/resource/nicene-marks-post-christendom-church/.

61. This reflected in the recent international Lutheran-Catholic study document, *The Apostolicity of the Church* (2006), where apostolic is defined as "an attribute effected by the Holy Spirit who unites, sanctifies, and maintains believers over time in continuity with the apostles' faith, teaching, and institutional order." *The Apostolicity of the Church: Study Document of the Lutheran-Roman Catholic Commission on Unity*, The Lutheran World Federation and Pontifical Council for Promoting Christian Unity (Minneapolis: Lutheran University Press, 2006), 47.

62. Carl E. Braaten, *Principles of Lutheran Theology*, 2d ed. (Minneapolis: Fortress Press, 2007), 62.

63. *BC*, 439.

64. The Lutherans would affirm the catholicity of the church apart from Roman obedience, arguing that there could only be one universal church spreading throughout the world because there could be only one true faith and therefore only one church in which that faith was confessed and believed. The church was catholic insofar as it was faithful to this one gospel attested by Scripture and early Christian fathers. See Dulles, *Catholicity of the Church*, 148.

65. Conrad Bergendoff, *The One, Holy, Catholic, and Apostolic Church*, The Hoover Lectures 1953 (Rock Island, IL: Augustana Book Concern, 1954), 51.

66. Edmund Schlink, "The Holy Spirit and Catholicity: A Report on Section 1 of the Uppsala Assembly," *Ecumenical Review* 21, no. 2 (1969): 102.

67. Darrell L. Guder, ed., *Missional Church: A Vision for the Sending of the Church in North America* (Grand Rapids: Eerdmans, 1998), 257.

68. Ibid.

69. Dulles, *Catholicity of the Church*, 180.

70. Guder, *Missional Church*, 257.

71. Robert J. Schreiter writes of the "narrative of the lie," regarding how violence is used to destroy the narratives that sustain a people's identity. "These might be called the narratives of the lie, precisely because they are intended to negate the truth of people's own narratives. . . . The negation is intended not only to destroy the narrative of the victim, but to pave the way for the oppressor's narrative." Schreiter, *Reconciliation: Mission and Ministry in a Changing Social Order* (Maryknoll, NY: Orbis, 1992), 34.

72. *BC*, 438.

73. Braaten, *Principles of Lutheran Theology*, 68. It should not amaze the media when Christians offer forgiveness in the face of deep pain and suffering, as happened when the Amish community in Nickel Mines, Pennsylvania, reacted to a horrible act of violence against their community that left five dead and as many severely injured. Charles Gibson, "Amish Say They 'Forgive' School Shooter." ABC News, October 3, 2006, http://abcnews.go.com/WNT/story?id=2523941&page=1.

Epilogue: A Vision for Revival

The crisis facing the mainline churches today is not one of survival, but one of ecclesial identity. It therefore will not be solved by new strategies or programs, but by reclaiming a theological identity for the church today. The purpose of this book has been to consider theological starting points for this task and to propose one way forward: that the church's identity is best rediscovered by considering the narrative of the church and that this story properly "starts with the Spirit."

If Nicholas Healy is correct that that the purpose of ecclesiology is not in finding the "right way" to think about the church, or in "developing a blueprint suitable for all times and places," then ecclesiology should support the "concrete church" in its ministry and mission.[1] My hope is that pastors and other theological leaders in the church will find, in this approach to ecclesiology, some new perspectives to help them and their congregations see (and hear) their life and ministry in light of what God the Holy Spirit is doing in and through them. Inevitably, however, when I have presented these ideas to groups of pastors, questions are raised regarding their implementation: What might this look like in my congregation? How do we put these ideas into practice? In other words, how does one translate the theological ideas of this book into the rhythm of life in an average mainline congregation?

For reasons that I hope are clear by now, I will offer neither a "plan for survival" nor a strategy or step-by-step plan for how to turn your congregation into a "Spirit-breathed" community. As I have argued throughout the book, the church is not created by human activities, but by the activity of the Holy Spirit through word and sacrament. A few years ago, I had a conversation with a Lutheran Reformation scholar who was adamantly against "missional" language and anything that suggested a "missional" approach to ministry. For him, it seemed like another version of works righteousness. He was hearing a message like this: if the church is not being "missional," it is not being the church—and further, this is something we can fix, by doing "missional" activities. The point here is not, "Do these things, *and then* you will be the church," but rather, "You *are* the church, so *be* the church!" The question "Who is the church?" leads not to a prescribed set of activities, but to a rediscovery and reclamation of (or better yet, *a being reclaimed by*) the biblical identity that God has bestowed on the church as a Spirit-breathed people. The Spirit enables the church both to receive the gospel promise of forgiveness of sins and live it out (albeit quite imperfectly) in a *koinonia* of relationships that is extended to the wider community, and leads the church outward, sharing this gospel in word and deed with a broken world.

Instead of a "plan for survival," I offer here a "vision for revival." I am not trying to be provocative in my use of the word *revival*, which I realize will raise more than a few Lutheran and Reformed eyebrows.[2] My purpose in using this term is simply to retrieve its most basic meaning, that is, to "bring back to life." Specifically, what might it look like for the mainline churches to be revived by the Spirit and live into a Spirit-breathed identity?

One could approach this task through sociological or ethnographic studies of local congregations who have rediscovered a theological identity and have found ways to live that identity out in specific ways and concrete practices. The work of Diana Butler Bass comes to mind here, especially *Christianity for the Rest of Us.*[3] This approach goes beyond the boundaries of this book (though I welcome other scholars taking up the project), but has some limitations as a resource for pastors and congregational leaders. First, as some of my former students note, lifting up examples of what is "working in other places" can often evoke a sense of guilt or even shame in pastors instead of inspiration to "go and do likewise."[4] Second, even when so inspired, difficulties often arise when leaders take something that works well in one congregational setting and try to duplicate it in another setting because of differences in personalities, history, and context. Here I will offer a snapshot of one congregation and some reflections on how pastors and other leaders can use narrative to help congregations reclaim and live into their Spirit-breathed identity.

In the foreword to Pastor Rick Barger's *A New and Right Spirit: Creating an Authentic Church in a Consumer Culture,*[5] Mark Allan Powell tells the story of how Abiding Hope Lutheran Church in Littleton, Colorado, made the news when they were among those first on the scene to respond pastorally to the shootings at Columbine High School in 1999:

> What the media missed was that long before the Columbine shootings, Abiding Hope Lutheran Church was a congregation of people who were genuinely excited over God raising Jesus from the dead. . . . The real story of Abiding Hope is not what happened in 1999 but what happens every Sunday of the year. One gets a

sense of this story simply by walking into the sanctuary any time the congregation gathers. These people are passionate about Jesus, and as a congregation they get what faith is all about. It's about God (not them); it's about Jesus Christ, whom God raised from the dead.

Powell goes on to say that this "right spirit" is what people first notice when they attend Abiding Hope, "not programs or mission directives, but a spirit of life that arises from what God did on Easter morning."[6]

I often ask groups of pastors: When visitors attend a Sunday morning service in your congregation, what do they first notice? Do they see simply another voluntary association, a group of people bonded by a common purpose and history, looking for volunteers for one activity or another, trying to get people to join their organization—a place where "God is conspicuously absent?" What if, instead, they saw (even dimly) a people who believe that Jesus Christ was raised from the dead—and that is what makes all the difference? That the same Spirit who raised Jesus from the dead is raising them to new life—a life that is to be shared with the world? How might a congregation begin to reclaim this biblical identity for itself?

As I have shown, the biblical narrative of the church in the Acts of the Apostles moves from death to new life, from fear to freedom. The first place one might begin, then, is with *what needs to die:* the concept of the church as a voluntary association. Having served for twelve years as a parish pastor, I am aware of how difficult it is to move people away from this church concept and into new ways of thinking about the church. It will not happen overnight. It will require using new language for speaking about the church. One might begin by eliminating the word *volunteer* from your vocabulary whenever speaking about the church. Volunteers volunteer for voluntary associations. Disciples of Jesus offer themselves to the Holy Spirit to be used for the mission of God; they offer the gifts with which God has blessed the church. Instead of volunteering our time, talents, and money, a Spirit-breathed church would pray for the Holy Spirit to equip disciples with the spiritual gifts needed to empower the church for its ministry to the neighborhood and the world.[7]

Second, narrative can be used in very practical ways in the parish to help members think in new ways about *who the church is* through Scripture study, preaching, and liturgy. The resources for reclaiming a Spirit-breathed identity for the church are found right at our fingertips: in our Bibles, our creeds, and our hymnals. Barger, now pastor at Epiphany Lutheran Church in Suwanee,

Georgia, developed a study that draws on Acts to help move members from the "old script" to a "new script."[8] He still uses a version of this study in new-member classes, "Discovering the Church Again for the First Time," but such a study could also be used as a midweek or Sunday study for congregational members, or as the "devotion" portion of a monthly church council or vestry meeting (which then can set the tone for the "business" portion of the meeting). The goal is to help members reflect on how the biblical story intersects with the story of their congregation—and the stories of its members. One pastor I know teaches members of his congregation to read Scripture "through the lens of participating in God's mission" by reflecting on questions such as: What is God doing in this story? What does this tell me about who God is? What does this tell me about who God is calling me to be? Where do I see a similar scenario in my life, relationships, world, etc.? How can I participate in Jesus' mission with respect to those situations? Many pastors I know use narrative preaching to model this engagement between the story in the text and the story of their lives.[9]

We are all familiar with congregations who are good at telling the story of their congregational or denominational history. The challenge is how to begin telling their congregational story as part of a larger story—the story of how the Spirit has guided this congregation to bear the gospel in this place, this neighborhood. The congregation I served in Milwaukee, as the oldest Lutheran congregation in the city, was proud of their history and celebrated their anniversary every year. In recent decades, they learned how to tell their story in light of what God was doing through them in the present—not just the past. Their story began with the arrival of German immigrants in the mid-nineteenth century—but expanded to include a ministry to newer immigrants from Laos.

Third, as members become immersed in and identify with this new biblical narrative, it is important for them to learn how to share this story with others, for we are called to be witnesses "of these things" (Acts 1:18). In other words, we need to learn to evangelize, to share with others what God is up to in our lives and in the world. This includes learning to share the hope that is within us (1 Peter 3:15) but also to point to the signs of the resurrection wherever we see them in our midst. This requires being more attentive to what the Holy Spirit is already at work doing in your congregation (and neighborhood) to make Christ known. One pastor started his ministry at a new congregation three years ago by asking members to tell him where they saw Jesus recently. At first, he said, they were dumbfounded by the question, but after they realized he was not going to stop asking it, they began to look for—and see—Jesus in their midst in terms of signs of God's reign, healing, and reconciliation, and the fruits of the Spirit. He has developed a discipleship peer-coaching model where members learn to become evangelists by sharing with each other where they have seen Jesus. Craig Nessan has suggested that Lutherans and other mainline Christians need to reclaim the art of "speaking the faith" to one another in order to be become evangelizers of the gospel to others, including testimony in worship.[10]

This leads to my final point: a Spirit-breathed church will reflect the experience of new life that the Holy Spirit brings in and through us. While this new life is something God brings about and not something we manufacture through our own activity, the Spirit calls us to be more intentional about how we reflect it in our life together, as a people who are both gathered and sent. How we live as God's people is often a more powerful witness than what we profess as God's people. Specifically, we can become more attentive and open to the movement of the Holy Spirit in how we both receive and offer the forgiveness of sins, how we participate in community, and how/where we are sent out in the mission of God in the world.[11]

Who is the church? The church is a Spirit-breathed people who learn to embody the promise of the forgiveness of sins in its own communal life (imperfectly as no doubt will be the case). The church is a Spirit-breathed people who are formed by the word and sacrament around which they gather weekly to become a *koinonia* of sharing and healing. The church is a Spirit-breathed people who are sent out into the world to share God's forgiveness and *koinonia* with a hurting and broken world.

For Reflection and Discussion

1. What would it be like to walk into a congregation's Sunday-morning worship service and be struck with the realization that "These people really believe that Jesus Christ rose from the dead—and that makes all the difference!"? What would it be like to be part of such a congregation?

2. What in your congregation needs to die before new life can fully emerge?

3. What story (or stories) is being told in your congregation? Who is at the center of this story? How do we begin to tell those stories in light of story of God's mission?

4. How do people in your congregation learn to tell "the old, old story?" Have you experimented with the suggestions given above

(for example, giving testimony in Christian worship)? What has been the result?

Notes

1. Nicholas M. Healy, *Church, World, and the Christian Life: Practical-Prophetic Ecclesiology* (Cambridge: Cambridge University Press, 2000), 38.

2. Revivalism in America has frequently been nonsacramental, overly concerned with individual salvation, associated with "decision theology" and emotionalism, and often a lack of décor and good order.

3. Diana Butler Bass, *Christianity for the Rest of Us: How the Neighborhood Church Is Transforming the Faith* (San Francisco: HarperSanFrancisco, 2006).

4. See Karen A. McClintock, *Shame-Less Lives, Grace-Full Congregations* (Herndon, VA: Alban Institute, 2011),

5. Rick Barger, A *New and Right Spirit: Creating an Authentic Church in a Consumer Culture* (Herndon, VA: Alban Institute, 2005), vi–vii. Barger offers a vision of the church as an authentic community of the Spirit and discusses the kind of adaptive leadership required to lead a congregation into this vision.

6. Ibid., ix.

7. Membership language is also associated with voluntarism, but its biblical meaning could be reclaimed using the Pauline image of the body and the ways that the Spirit equips individual members of the body with spiritual gifts in order to build up the body for God's mission.

8. Rick Barger, "Witness to the Resurrection: A Biblical and Theological Symbol to Prepare Baby Boomers for Membership in the Growing, Suburban, Lutheran Congregation," DMin thesis, San Francisco Theological Seminary, 2001. See esp. 243–50.

9. One pastor recommends Donald Miller's *Storyline: Finding Your Subplot in God's Story* (Donald Miller Words, LLC, 2012) as a helpful resource; http://www.mystoryline.net/. Another recommends *The Narrative Lectionary*, begun by Rolf Jacobson and Craig Koester of Luther Seminary: www.workingpreacher.org/narrative.

10. Craig L. Nessan, *Beyond Maintenance to Mission: A Theology of the Congregation,* 2d ed. (Minneapolis: Fortress Press, 2010), 121–23. See also Frederick J. Gaiser, "'I will tell you what God has done for me' (Psalm 66:16): A Place for 'Testimony' in Lutheran Worship?" *Word & World* 26, no. 2 (2006): 138–48. One pastor recommends Martha Grace Reece's *Unbinding the Gospel: Real Life Evangelism*, with afterword by Brian McLaren (St. Louis: Chalice, 2007), and related resource at: http://www.gracenet.info/unbinding_the_gospel.aspx.

11. Many mainline Christians will need to become more comfortable with the language of the Spirit in order to do this. Here perhaps we could learn something from charismatic churches (such as the Vineyard Fellowship Church) who "expect God to show up" whenever they gather to worship and do ministry.

Index of Names and Subjects